the
happy
medium

SPEAKING THE LANGUAGE OF INTUITION

JODI LIVON

BEAVER'S POND
PRESS

Edited by Hanna Kjeldbjerg
Proofread by Alicia Ester

ISBN 13: 978-1-59298-748-1
Library of Congress Catalog Number: 2016917843

Printed in the United States of America
First Printing: 2016
20 19 18 17 16   5 4 3 2 1

Photographs by Taylor Tupy
Book design and typesetting by Athena Currier

THE HAPPY MEDIUM is a trademark of Jodi Livon

Beaver's Pond Press
7108 Ohms Lane
Edina, MN 55439–2129
(952) 829-8818
www.BeaversPondPress.com

To order, visit www.ItascaBooks.com
or call (800)-901-3480. Reseller discounts available.

To contact Livon for speaking engagements, online classes, private readings, or corporate coaching, visit her online at www.theintuitivecoach.com

Praise for *The Happy Medium:*
Speaking the Language of Intuition

"Livon skillfully teaches how to release our innate intuition through the highest vibration—the vibration of love."

—Adrian Finkelstein, MD, author of *By Love Reclaimed*

"Jodi Livon is one of the most engaging and entertaining speakers, and a truly talented and compassionate medium. Her new book, *The Happy Medium: Speaking the Language of Intuition*, gives insight into the mystery and enigma of intuition from a fun and relatable point of view. She is the teacher we all have been waiting for!"

—Dave Schrader, co-host of the paranormal radio show *Darkness On The Edge Of Town*

"Jodi Livon's expertise and positivity shine in each illuminating chapter of *The Happy Medium: Speaking the Language of Intuition*. Use this book to activate your intuition today!"

—Annie Wilder, author of *House of Spirits and Whispers* and *Spirits Out of Time*

"JODI LIVON IS THE REAL DEAL. Her teachings are a treasure to those of us interested in exploring and deepening our spiritual gifts. If you're looking for a wise, authentic, straightforward tour guide to your unique intuitive landscape, look no further than Jodi."

—Tess Whitehurst, author of *The Good Energy Book: Creating Harmony and Balance for Yourself and Your Home* and *Magical Housekeeping: Simple Charms and Practical Tips for Creating a Harmonious Home*

"JODI HAS DONE IT AGAIN! This book, like its author, is able to open pathways to your intuition. I am truly appreciative of her talents to teach others to trust themselves."

—Laura Evans, medium and founder of the Zenith School of Metaphysical Studies

"JODI LIVON'S WARMTH AND NATURAL TALENT as a medium and teacher radiantly shine through in *The Happy Medium: Speaking the Language of Intuition*. Her wealth of intuitive wisdom is so needed in these times of change. This book will help you move through life with confidence and grace."

—Kari Samuels, intuitive counselor and happiness coach

"JODI LIVON IS A DYNAMITE TV PERSONALITY and an incredible author. She has a way of breaking down the intuitive process into something nearly everyone can understand. She's mystical without being mysterious. *The Happy Medium: Speaking the Language of Intuition* is beautifully written and filled with invaluable insight!"

—Amanda Tadych, Executive Producer, *Twin Cities Live, 5 Eyewitness News* | KSTP-TV, LLC

This book is lovingly dedicated to my beautiful family, Jason, Cole, Aaron, and Sophia Rein.

Love and intuition are both the language of the soul. Speak soul.

Contents

Foreword

My longtime friendship with Jodi Livon has been among the most rewarding of my life. Aside from sharing her gifts of warmth, humor, generosity, and integrity, Jodi has convinced me, beyond all reasonable doubt, that evidential mediumship—and the eternal life to which it points—is a reality.

She is a medium and spiritual teacher par excellence. I acknowledge unabashedly that it is quite likely I will be forever in her debt.

Jodi's first book, *The Happy Medium: Awakening to Your Natural Intuition*, is a best-selling gem, and in the pages of her second book you will find clear signs of a steady progression in her own spiritual evolution. Each page offers encouraging insights and a gentle lesson that points the way to accelerated soul growth. All of that is owing to Jodi's willingness to tend her own garden before advising others, and her principled refusal to underestimate the serious business of personal development.

Her decades of accumulated wisdom are now in your hands. Read with expectancy and practice with joy. You will love where *The Happy Medium: Speaking the Language of Intuition* takes you!

Gary Mantz
Co-host of *Mantz & Mitchell*, KKNW Seattle

Preface

Not Everything Is Black and White

After my first book, I thought I would write another book about happiness because I was having so much fun being happy. I thought I would write a how-to book about the intricacies of utilizing intuition because I wanted to help people experience the wealth of guidance and joy available to them. I thought and felt and sensed and wrote. And then I fell.

Following the August 2009 launch of my first book, *The Happy Medium: Awakening to Your Natural Intuition*, I was swept away in a fast-moving current. Over three hundred people attended the launch party, and the store sold a record number of books. I thought it was a sign of love and support from friends, family, and clients. As it turns out, it was, but as *The Happy Medium* propelled me into a completely new realm, I realized it was also a sign of the times.

Following my debut appearance on a popular local television show, *Twin Cities Live*, I was invited to return every week the following month. That month turned into a regular gig. Since August 2009, I've been the resident psychic on KSTP's *Twin Cities Live* and have been showcasing the beauty of the intuitive process by reading people, animals, and national celebrities, along with doing ghost investigations of local and national hot spots.

There is no question—people are interested in seeing the natural intuitive process in living color! They're also interested in reading about it in books because it validates their own perceptions. It's not about being spooked or even entertained. It's about understanding that not everything is black and white.

On a personal level, I was enjoying the process of creating a fulfilling reality and all the benefits that come with it. It's not that there weren't the usual ups and downs; it's that I constantly practiced picking myself up and moving forward. And as an intuitive coach in the corporate world and private sector, I made a living coaching other people to do the same.

As a medium, I can sense the energy of those on the other side. I interpret the images that my guides and those in spirit drop onto the screen in my head. This type of work can make a huge difference because it helps my clients find what belongs to them: closure and inner peace.

I traveled a long way to be able to cleanly and clearly do the work I do. Building and maintaining decent boundaries has been key. Being highly sensitive, a.k.a. intuitive, comes naturally to me. Unlike some of the other reputable psychics and mediums I've met, I had to learn to turn the stream of information that floods me way down, not up!

Now that I have a solid understanding of how the intuitive process works to advance and enhance my life I can't imagine living without it. Living intuitively is central to my life. And everyone has this cool intuitive ability—*everyone.* Yes, it's true that some have more capacity than others. We are all psychic, of course, but creative folks have more access to their insights because they work intentionally through the energy of inspiration. Highly creative people work more consciously through their souls.

The connection with the higher soul leads us to the Divine. Here is where the Universal Bank of Knowledge awaits. The key to receiving information, intuitively speaking, is connecting with our mind, body, and spirit.

The line connecting to the Universal Bank of Knowledge must be clear to be effective. *We are the line.*

So when I experienced a series of losses, when they proved far more difficult for me than they ever had before, when I found myself falling, I did what I've always done to heal my heart: I leaned on my intuition. And I wrote.

The Grace of Colleen

None of us is immune to misfortune—it dots everyone's life and usually happens more than once. Obviously I'm a big proponent of trusting my intuition. And believe me, my intuition earned the trust. When my gut leads me somewhere, I check in with my head and heart. When all three are in alignment I move forward. Or in this case, I moved.

My husband Jason and I made the decision to move based on the educational needs of our children, as well as in reaction to a number of signs—lightning severely damaging our house three times, dreams indicating a move closer to water, and a sinking feeling in my gut whenever I thought of staying in our home, even though it was adorable and we had wonderful friends in the area. We sold our home only to find that the house we hoped to purchase failed a crucial moisture test. Then the next four houses we put offers on proved to have a similar problem, so we widened our search to include cities we had always admired but felt were too far away. We had to be out of our home in less than a month and with school starting in a matter of weeks, we still didn't know which district we would be in.

All of this was confusing to me because I had followed what I knew to be so solid—my instincts—and yet at every turn, things became worse. I found myself filling with self-doubt.

At the same time this was happening, Colleen, one of my dearest friends who lived minutes from my now-sold pretty brown brick house, fell ill. Very ill. Weeks before, her white blood cell count had been a bit high. When she went in a second time it was alarmingly high, and she was immediately checked in to the hospital. Within hours, all test results pointed toward leukemia.

Colleen and I had always spent a lot of time together, but since I entered house-hunting hell, my time had been limited. Besides feeling an uncommon distance between us, I had received no intuitive heads-up that she was ill. I did not sense the presence of cancer. Cue more self-doubt. And more than a few moments of tremendous guilt.

What helps me find balance now is when I remember that the Universe is full and wise. Information is given to us or held back for reasons we may not understand until we ourselves are on the other side.

My focus had drastically shifted away from wanting to move. But our house was sold, so we had to find a home. My time was split between searching for a house and spending time with Colleen. While I tried to stay calm in the wake of her family's storm, I selfishly felt like someone had picked up my life, turned it upside down, and shook furiously.

When I think of strong women, Colleen's gorgeous face always comes to mind. Even now, years later, I find it difficult to refer to her in past tense. Her amazing family and friends stepped forward while—true to form—she fought like a warrior. Despite the best of efforts, my warrior friend died. She died as she had lived: with grace.

The way her husband, Harlan, is dealing with her death and finding a new kind of life is a marvel. Clearly he and his children are heartrendingly sad, but they continue to look forward rather than backward.

In the end, Jason and I found a beautiful home in an outstanding community. Our wonderful neighbors quickly became our friends. Nevertheless, my reaction to losing one of my closest friends and moving away from my community surprised me. Emotionally I fell down, which wasn't a shock; but I didn't care to get up, which was.

At one point, shortly after Colleen died, I was driving down an icy road and a truck nearly slid into the driver's side of my car. I heard myself say, *Wow, that truck could have killed me,* and I noticed with a shudder that I didn't care as much as I should have. Shock ran through me as I recognized I was depressed.

I knew the pain I was feeling was the flip side of my joy, and if only I could find my groove I would naturally be able to reclaim my poise and self-confidence. I'd been lost before, but this combination of events was one for the books. Or at least a book! I wrote down some of the foremost remedy-like intuition building exercises I shared with clients, along with every other positive ingredient I knew would help me raise my spirit and find my happy. I poured every problem-solving, vibe-boosting, insight-building, silly, private, mystic stimulant I knew onto the pages and collapsed into the words.

This may not be the book that I originally imagined myself writing, but *The Happy Medium: Speaking the Language of Intuition* has turned out to be so much more. Give these artful exercises a try, sharpen your intuitive eye, and find your own happy!

Introduction

My first book, *The Happy Medium: Awakening to Your Natural Intuition*, validated the existence of life after life and the beauty of the intuitive process. *The Happy Medium: Speaking the Language of Intuition* puts that message into practice to offer vibrant, appealing, intuition-boosting exercises that will help you become more of your intuitive-happy self.

For centuries musicians, philosophers, poets, and the like have searched for the key to happiness with as much passion as the many scientists who study energy in its countless forms. What's interesting is that happiness *is* an actual energy. If only they had all gotten together and read the Winnie-the-Pooh books by A. A. Milne, they may have found their answers neatly tucked within the pages.

Do you remember Eeyore, the cynical character in the Winnie-the-Pooh books? He's Winnie-the-Pooh's ever-glum, satirical, and doubtful donkey friend. In his eyes, nothing ever goes right, so as "luck" would have it, nothing much does.

And then there's Pooh's enthusiastic, energetic, optimistic—yet less-than-responsible—mischief-making tiger friend, Tigger. He loves to bounce around and thinks that whatever he does, he does best. He's happy-go-lucky, and so as "luck" would have it, things repeatedly turn out well for him.

It's true that *what we see is what we get*. This is not only a mind-set—it's an energy set. Our "luck" is simply a manifestation of our vibrational energy frequency. Our vibrational frequency is the level at which we radiate. It's the vibe we *radiate*. A feeling of happiness denotes a high energy, or a raised vibration. It's a Tigger-kind-of-feeling thing. In actuality, what we *see*, what we *say*, and what we *think* is what we *get*!

Eeyore doesn't think positively, see the good, or radiate joy, so he vibrates at a lower frequency. As a result, good things don't seem to drop into his lap which, of course, supports his pessimistic attitude, which brings on more of the same.

Optimistic Tigger, on the other hand, radiates joy, so his vibration is raised and his life is filled with opportunity. He clearly appreciates the "good stuff" and so has more of it.

When we are higher in frequency, we're higher in consciousness, so we can connect to our higher soul-self, which is the *enlightened* part of us. Our vibration is not about *who* we are, it is about *how* we are. Sporting a raised vibration not only brings us more joy (and all sorts of goodies!), it connects us with that big, beautiful Universal Bank of Knowledge and *voilà,* we are aware of, and awake to, our psychic soul-self, and the strength of our intuitive voice is amplified!

Each soul is a spark that is connected to the One Universal Light, a.k.a. G-d, Universe, or Source. In this light, everything looks brighter, more brilliant, and dazzling! Instinctively, we all recognize this as truth. Like a homing device, the soul *can* find its way to that connection. We just have to let our soul do its thing. We have to jump on our high-flying vibe.

That's where *The Happy Medium: Speaking the Language of Intuition* comes in with chapters and exercises such as "Trust Your Gut, Not Your Guilt," "Reaching through

the Veil," and "Triggering Numbers, Symbols, and Signs."
They are fun to do, which brings joy and raises our vibration—making us not only more intuitive, but more likely
to attract the good stuff in life!

These vibrant intuition-boosting practices will significantly increase your rate of accurate insights. Steady
use of these exercises will help you live big, teaching you to
use every bit of your natural intuition to successfully flow
through life and live in a place of abundance, acceptance,
and soul.

Every soul sparkles, and to connect with the soul is
to feel that sparkle. My intuitive abilities have wholly enriched my capacity to do so. It is truly an honor and a
privilege to help you spark your own!

Prologue

When Things Don't Add Up, Intuition Helps You Do the Math

The blood drained from my face, my stomach heaved, and I wanted to throw up, preferably all over Mr. Nova's shoes. But I stood tall and curly and kept trying to make sense of the numbers that seemed to move across the board. It was half past twelve, fifteen minutes until lunchtime, and there were only seven people left standing.

Our sixth-grade math teacher, Mr. Nova, had lined up our entire class at the board to finish our individual math problems. He said we could not go to lunch until every single one of us had completed the task. Ten minutes later I was the only one left standing. Mr. Nova approached me *again,* his ugly brown Hush Puppies tapping to the beat of the large hand on the clock. If it was at all possible, I was becoming even less confident with each passing ticktock. At that moment, I was no doubt his biggest problem, and my hungry classmates probably felt the same.

My biggest problem at the moment was dyslexia. I've struggled with it all my life. Doing math poses a special hurdle. My brain doesn't recognize and process certain symbols. My processing speed—well, isn't speedy. I sporadically reverse numbers and letters.

Ticktock went the clock and then something clicked in my head, or rather my gut! I watched from a distance as my hand seemed to move by itself to the blackboard. The chalk resting in my fingers quickly pounded out five numbers. There, in black and white, was the answer. Mr. Nova walked slowly over and eyed the numbers. He looked for the mathematical jargon that typically accompanies long math but there was none. He turned quickly and asked the class if someone had helped me. No one said a word. He asked me how I had arrived at the answer. I looked him in the eye and then down at my baggy green corduroy pants that seemed to pool on top of my Adidas tennis shoes.

If I had magical powers I would have waved my hand and disappeared. Or I would have turned Mr. Nova into one of my classmates' sweaty gym socks, but just for an afternoon. He wasn't all bad, but he sure was mad at me. I was hungry and absolutely humiliated. I had two choices that day: to cry, which seemed imminent, or to show my teacher what I knew. I chose the latter. It was all there, written in white chalk. But he wanted more.

What was I going to tell him—that I was an overly skinny, insecure, buck-toothed, supernatural, and super-weird superstar? Or the truth—that the still, small voice inside of me came to the rescue, *once again*. He wouldn't believe me. No one had ever believed me. Not that I had overshared.

I would need to do some long, very long math to count how many times my intuition rescued me during childhood. But there was a flip side. Wayward spirits always had a field day with me. Turning lights off and on, tossing objects across the room, and hiding my hairbrush and ponytail holders were the least of it. The things that went *boo* in the night followed me around during the day.

At home, the message was clear: I was to *say nothing* about knowing personal information about pretty much everyone, including ghosts. Now at the chalkboard, I just stood there, my face turning a deeper shade of red with each passing second. I don't know if Mr. Nova took pity on me or was just too starved to insist I respond. He turned away and excused the class for lunch.

During my sixth-grade math saga I didn't realize I was calming my mind to gain access to my intuition. Had anyone known, my reputation as *weird* would have been turned up several notches! But learning to use our intuition doesn't have to feel weird. It's more about how we all already use it, and how easy it is to expand that capability.

Our intuition is not acquired; it is inherent. As newborns, we instinctively know how to breathe and how to cry. In the same way, we also are quietly aware of the whisper of internal signals we call intuition, but unless they are unusually loud, like mine were, we unconsciously begin to ignore them.

But by doing certain exercises, our thinking is renovated and we naturally begin to restore the connection. *The Happy Medium: Speaking the Language of Intuition* is filled with these powerful, yet simple tools, techniques, and exercises. You hold, and have always held, your own means to a priceless piece of bliss. Welcome back to your inheritance, your birthright, your own intuition.

Chapter 1

The Language of Intuition

Your feelings are the wings of your intuition.

Your intuitive voice speaks a language unique to your own spirit. Believe it or not, you already understand much of it—you know it by heart and *soul!*

A language is simply a method of communication. Humans communicate in many different ways—in fact, there are over 6,500 languages spoken in the world today. But everyone, and I do mean everyone, communicates through intuition. And that is how those on the other side of the veil communicate with us, as well.

The language of intuition involves a kind of code—an intuitive code. Its signals are communicated through emotions and physical sensations. *Deciphering what these sensations mean is the key to understanding the language of intuition.* Since sensations are really feelings, and emotions are the story you tell yourself about what your feelings mean, learning the language of intuition comes down to one single factor: feelings.

Most of us ignore our feelings because they seem like a lot to deal with. We do not have control over our feelings, nor should we try. But what we must remember is, complex or welcomed, our feelings are a gift from the Universe and how we honor them is our gift back.

When we honor them, discerning signals will begin to come naturally. For example, clamminess and cold chills are not just signs of the flu—they can be intuitive signals to be alert. In a similar way, that feeling of butterflies in the tummy is not always nerves—it could be a sign something special is taking wing in your life. But you won't be able to read these signs if you have shut down emotionally.

Since the language of intuition speaks through feelings, and feelings incorporate senses, a good question to ask is, "What is my most receptive sense, or how am I most sensitive?" This is your deeper opening into the world of intuition and involves what I refer to as one of the Five Clairs.

The Five Clairs are clairvoyance (clear seeing, which is associated with the third eye), clairaudience (clear hearing), clairsentience (clear sensing or feeling, sometimes known as a gut instinct), clairallience (clear smelling), and clairgustance (clear tasting—yes, it's true, some psychics actually taste things intuitively!).

Snap your Clairs into action by becoming aware of the insightful messages delivered through them. For example, if you unexpectedly smell coffee brewing, and you are alone in your car without a drop nearby, your intuition may be speaking to you through your nose (clairallience)! Keep track of what this could mean by memorizing the feelings you had when you first smelled the coffee and wait patiently for the meaning to unfold.

Here's another example: let's say you won tickets to a fabulous show and have been wondering whom you should invite. All day long you have had the taste of cinnamon in your mouth, yet you have eaten none. Could this mean your taste buds are broken? Or is one of the Clairs, as in clairgustance, showing up with a message? *Well,* you think to yourself, *your dear friend Fred loves the theatre and regularly plays The Spice Girls. He's the friend to invite to the show!*

Or say that for the last two weeks your pen has gone missing after a Thursday work meeting. This Thursday is no different, and as you open up your drawer you promptly feel like someone has lightly kicked you in the ribs. Does this mean you are hungry? Or is it that your co-worker Sally was just talking about her pregnancy, and how *she can now feel her baby kick*? Sally, who happens to be the manager of those meetings, where there are always pens available for use. And now that you think of it, they look suspiciously like the ones you buy. This is dear Clair, as in clairsentience, at work.

When you are aware of how you feel, you become more intuitive in general.

Let's look at it a different way. Do you remember the game Operation? The game consists of an "operating table" lithographed with a funny likeness of a patient whose name is Cavity Sam. Sam has several cavity openings on his body exposing silly ailments made of plastic, like a small horse resting near the hip joint to signify a charley horse. The overall gameplay entails players removing these plastic "disorders" with a pair of tweezers, all without touching the edge of the cavity opening. If a player touches the edge, the large red lightbulb on Cavity Sam's nose blinks and a buzzer sounds. As a way of tossing some humor on the whole tendency to *ignore our feelings*, let's play an intuitive game, using the idea of Operation!

Tools & Techniques
Give Your Intuition a Buzz

Who—YOU
What—Awakening to intuitive signals
When—You have a few hours away from work
Where—You are free to pause and take in your feelings

Begin this exercise by sitting with legs and arms uncrossed. Slowly raise your hands up and reach for the sky. Bring them back down and rub your palms together until you feel them become warm. Now rest your hands on your thighs with palms facing up. Gently close your eyes and listen to the sound of your breath as you slowly inhale and exhale three times through your nose. Feel the rise and fall of your belly as you breathe and relax into the flow of air as it moves through you.

- Continue breathing, knowing that your feelings are your friends. They are the wings of your intuition, and show you where you need to go to grow your soul. Consciously agree to honor your feelings and strengthen your connection with your inner voice.

- Imagine turning the game *on*, and then get up and start moving through your day.

- As you become aware of your feelings, place them into one of two categories—*fear* or *love*. Imagine the pleasant sound of a flute playing when a loving feeling comes up and a faint, but noticeable, blink of red light when you feel fear.

- You will be surprised at how often you actually feel something. Welcome the knowledge—you are awakening to your natural intuition. The more aware you are, the more intuitive you become.

- Notice if you see red or hear music when you meet someone new or encounter a situation you were not expecting. Acknowledge that fear is not bad—it is only a signal to look further and deeper.

- Start noticing how your body feels. When you feel fear, how does it feel? How is it different from when you feel love? When you notice how your feelings *feel* you honor them and begin to understand your own intuitive code.

- At the end of the exercise, imagine clicking the *off* button on the game. The red light and flute are no longer necessary, but the exercise is available at your will.

Acknowledging your feelings is paramount to understanding the language of intuition. Once you have that down, you have cracked a major part of the code, and can begin to truly listen to and use your intuition.

Chapter 2

Gratitude and Light

*When we are filled with light
we become the light.*

Have you ever met someone whose very presence makes you feel at peace? They can find an answer to any problem, big or small, seemingly without much effort. They appear naturally joyful, and good luck seems to follow them. It's almost as if they radiate calmness—they flow.

What you're noticing in these people is a high vibrational frequency. A vibrational frequency, or *vibe*, is the speed at which the atoms and subatomic particles of an object or organism vibrate. It's the level at which we *radiate.* When we're in a bad mood, our vibrational frequency is low. When we're in a good mood, we are higher in frequency, and higher in consciousness. Higher frequency and higher consciousness truly go hand in hand. Our vibration is not about *who* we are, it's actually *how* we are!

Remember optimistic, joy-radiating Tigger from the Winnie-the-Pooh books? Well, Tigger sports a high vibe, and is grateful and filled with light. Perhaps he knows that *what we see is what we get.* He sees the good, so has more of it. This is not only a mind-set, it's truly an energy set. His "good luck" is simply a manifestation of his high vibrational frequency. It's simple. Seeing things in a positive light *creates more light.* It's not about a glass half empty or half full, it's about feeling happy no matter how full the glass is.

We can create this perspective by consciously noticing something, anything, that legitimately brings us joy in each moment. When we are in a place of appreciation, we are connected to our higher soul-self and the Universe. And *connected* is where we want to be. Our spirit naturally wants to be closer to the Universe, and when we vibrate at a high speed we are.

The key to receiving information, intuitively speaking, is that connection, which allows us to access the Universal Bank of Knowledge—where we go for glimpses of what was, what is, and what may be. When our frequencies are high we are super-psychic and automatically act on our intuitive impulses. We have more "out-of-the-blue" urges to call someone or act on a hunch, and that action leads to something meaningful. We also seem to be in "the right place at the right time" nearly all the time. It's about the vibe.

The voice of our intuition, as you know, operates through our *feelings*. And when we are aware of our feelings *and* stand in a place of gratitude, our insights become amplified and are no longer a whisper.

When we begin to tune into our intuition, it almost feels like stepping into a whole new world. Imagine riding in an elevator all the way to the top floor of a magnificently built high rise. Once the elevator doors open, you are enveloped in warm yellow light pouring in from the floor-to-ceiling windows, and you feel filled with love. You wonder why you spent so many years on the lower floors when this incredible view was here all along, and the moment the question forms in your mind, the answer is provided through a *strong sense of knowing*—that you arrived at exactly the right time. In fact, as you continue to fill yourself with gratitude for being gifted with this beautiful view of the world, you continue to be presented with insights. The vibration of appreciation is that powerful.

Elevating your vibration is like taking that elevator ride to the top floor. Always remember that changing your words changes your mind. Changing your mind alters your energy, and that is what changes your life.

In this exercise, let's practice how to achieve your own Tigger-kind-of-feeling space by adjusting the way you see your world. The goal is to find something you like everywhere you look. What you see—and say, for that matter—is what you get, meaning you will get more of the same!

Tools & Techniques
What We See Is What We Get

Who—Everyone interested in significantly grow-
ing their intuition through "good luck"
What—Raising your vibe through appreciation
When—Begin prior to starting your day and
continue throughout
Where—At work, at home, at school, during drive-
time—everywhere

Start this exercise by sitting or standing with spine
straight and legs and arms uncrossed. A straight back
means you keep your spine tall without forcing it. Doing this opens you up spiritually and energetically speaking. Gently close your eyes and listen to the sound of
your breath as you slowly inhale and exhale three times
through your nose. Feel the rise and fall of your belly
as you breathe and relax into the flow of air as it moves
through you.

Say your full name to yourself. Imagine a sparkling
white light moving simultaneously up from the core of the

earth and down from the heavens, touching and joining as they move through you. You are now divinely kissed. Everything you see is filled with this light.

Agree that for this day you will notice something that you truly like, love, or appreciate everywhere you go.

- Start in the morning by admiring and appreciating the sun as it peeks through your blinds.

- When you pass by a mirror, smile at yourself. Be love and light in action by loving and delighting in you!

- Each time you enter a new space find something in it that you like. Notice how you feel when you enter a room compared to how it feels after you've acknowledged what you enjoy about it.

- As you move through the day say, "I am a grateful, willing spirit with a balanced mind and an open heart."

- Acknowledge the love in everyone you see by saluting the spark in their soul.

- Put a positive spin on everything you say. If a negative statement escapes your lips, end it with, "And I know there is a more affirmative way of saying this and I'm getting there."

- If you are experiencing something that does not please you, be grateful that you are aware of it, and are not numb to your feelings.

- If you feel stuck on a project or problem, appreciate the challenge and acknowledge that at some point, you will conquer it.

- As the words you say and the thoughts you think elevate your vibe, transforming you into your intuitive-happy self, notice how *meaningful occurrences* appear to move in slow motion or are highlighted through depth of color. This is your intuition in action.

- As these serendipitous winks from the universe multiply, record them on your phone or in a notebook. When you notice that your questions, intuition-based or otherwise, are beginning to be answered, demonstrate appreciation by acknowledging it out loud or in your head.

- Speak words of affirmation as the day is ending. Give kudos to yourself, as well as to your children, spouse, and team members for their hard work.

What we see and say is what we get, so focus on the good and the good will multiply. The process is practically effortless and the outcome is amazing!

It's simple. Choose your words, choose your bliss! Seeing things in a positive light *creates more light,* which means we have the power to produce desirable outcomes. And that means more love, fun, and worldly goods—and more reveling in the bounty of life!

Chapter 3

Trust Your Gut, Not Your Guilt

I believe in the power of self-acceptance.
I am confident, strong, brave, and beautiful.

What is the difference between gut and guilt? Or more aptly put, a gut reaction and a guilt reaction? Guilt is an emotional reaction to our actions. On the other hand, a gut reaction is an intuitive or instinctual response. It's that knowing feeling, that *aha* moment, and that conscious awareness of truth.

Gut and guilt are *not* part of the same family. They don't even like each other!

Gut knows that guilt brings our energy down. And guilt is distrustful of gut's seemingly selfish motives, what with its encouragement to choose what is good for the soul and all.

One positive aspect of remorse is it provides an opportunity to take a deeper look at our actions so we can alter our choices to create healthier outcomes. However, guilt is frequently used as a tool for manipulation. When guilt is involved we feel ashamed and nothing feels good, sweet, or calm.

Our intuition works through feelings, so we know full well what an *off* or *bad* sensation is, and we know *bad* brings us down. When our vibe is down, we are no longer super-psychic, meaning we are not in our Tigger-kind-of-feeling space of appreciation, where we vibrate at a high speed and are connected to our higher soul-self and the Universe. Remember, the key to receiving information, intuitively speaking, is that connection.

My suggestion is that we look at guilt through an intuitive eye. When our gut intuition is involved, a peaceful, harmonious feeling permeates our senses and remains with us in relation to that particular choice. A gut-related reaction is peaceful, while a guilt-related reaction is prickly.

Save yourself a whole lot of time away from your warm, Tigger-kind-of-feeling space and learn to trust your gut, not your guilt. Here's how!

Tools & Techniques
Now-and-Later Decision Maker

Who—Everyone who occasionally makes decisions based
on guilt (so that means pretty much everyone)
What—Learn to make decisions based on gut intu-
ition instead of guilt trips
When—Absolutely anytime
Where—Absolutely anywhere

Stand or sit with spine straight and legs and arms uncrossed. Gently close your eyes and listen to the sound of your breath as you slowly inhale and exhale three times through your nose. Feel the rise and fall of your belly as you take in another breath, and relax into yourself as you exhale. Notice how your body feels as the flow of air moves through you.

Remember you are exactly where you need to be, and doing exactly what you need to do. The light that fills you from within is never dim. Every thought you think and choice you make is filled with this light.

Dial into a higher frequency by opening up to how you feel. Fill yourself with gratitude. This elevates the light from within and sharpens your intuitive eye. Set your intention by silently saying, "My choices are a reflection of my love of self. My love of self is a reflection of my connection with my soul and my Higher Power."

- Stand up and gently shake your hands out toward the ground.

- Take three slow, deep breaths through your nose, thinking about what decision requires your attention.

- Visualize the roots of a giant tree gently wrapping around your ankles and linking you to the earth. Breathe into this connection. Feel how safe and loved you are.

- Make an affirmative statement, either out loud or to yourself, such as, "I now choose to make personal decisions within the flow and grace of my intuitive instincts." (Read more about the use of affirmations in Chapter 13.)

- Quietly observe the potential choices and consider which decision will feel good both now *and* later when you reflect upon the matter.

- Contemplate one choice at a time and hold the decision in your thoughts.

- Notice precisely how you feel. For example, when you think about choosing what is *easiest,* but not healthy overall, what sensations arise?

- As you contemplate each choice, ask yourself, do you feel calm and peaceful? If so, you are making a decision based on gut. Do you feel irritable and prickly? If so, you are making a decision based on guilt.

- Always ask yourself if, given your choices, you will feel peaceful later. If your answer is yes, proceed!

- Notice how solutions find their way to you with little or no effort. When this happens, memorize the feeling you have at that moment. Next time you find yourself anxious about a problem, simply locate that same blissful feeling and breathe into it. This releases resistance, making it far easier for the solution to find you.

In matters of soul, business, family (or actually, simply everything!) there is nothing like trusting your gut, following your heart, and using your head. When all three are in alignment, there is steadiness. It's all about finding the happy medium. When you find that, you will have balance on your side. When love is involved, or rather, when *love of self* is involved, a decision that's based in guilt doesn't stand a chance.

Chapter 4

The Protection of Protection

*I am filled with a radiant white light and feel
present, peaceful, and prepared. I am alive to
this moment; this moment is all that is.*

Have you ever met a ghost you didn't like? Well I have—some
ghosts are bullies. I felt intimidated by the ferocious energy of
some of the earthbound spirits I encountered as a kid. What
I didn't know then was that this fear would be the impetus
I needed to stand up to bullies on both sides of the veil. I
guess I owe thanks to some of those spirits who, for whatever
reason, chose not to go into the light after their bodies died—
even if they did create quite the *atmosphere* in a room!

My biggest fear as a teen was that ghosts would follow me home and wrestle me out of my body so they could take over. Without proper boundaries I was vulnerable to misaligned energy in general. Because I didn't know how to keep my borders closed, so to speak, I was always picking up someone else's feelings and thinking they were my own, or worse, even picking up hitchhiker ghosts! It sounds scary (and it was) but it's over now that I learned to assert my boundaries.

Most people lack adequate boundaries and feel drained, in part, because of it. I speak at length about staying grounded and maintaining good boundaries in *The Happy Medium: Awakening to Your Natural Intuition*. It's a hot topic, and this time I'm covering the creation of healthy boundaries from a different angle to help decrease irritability and increase intuitive abilities so you can freely bounce yourself back into your intuitive-happy self!

Healthy boundaries protect you from energy that is not your own. It's fascinating to note that personal and psychic boundaries are actually one and the same. Decent boundaries are not only the foundation of intuitive work; they are, in my experience, the infrastructure of decent mental health.

To have good boundaries is to know where your space begins and ends. Knowing how you feel physically and emotionally provides solid support for this. If, out of the blue, your mood changes or you feel completely drained, you may have unconsciously allowed someone access to *your* space or you've wandered into *their* space through compassion, judgment, or curiosity.

No worries, though—there are ample techniques that can be applied to clear your space and help you stay in it. The key is staying grounded.

Being grounded is all about staying in the now, and being *consciously present in your body and connected to the earth*. That is why it's so powerful to visualize a cable, rope, or root of a tree connecting the base of your spine and the soles of your feet with the core of the earth. Just thinking about it grounds you!

Every breathing exercise and reference to white light in *The Happy Medium: Speaking the Language of Intuition* is centered on grounding and protection—which is exactly how you maintain boundaries. Think of having healthy boundaries as staying in your own lane while driving, keeping your eyes on your own paper when taking a test, and staying on your own mat while doing yoga!

Here are a few examples of how this works.

Say I'm decluttering my home and take a break to drop off seven giant bags of clothes and household items at a charity. I'm feeling exhausted, but good about the day, until I approach an unhappy worker who greets me with a grunt. I'm caught off guard by the heavy energy and, as a result, my own energy takes a nose dive. Even as I pull away I can't shake the murky dismay that now floods me.

What happened? My spirits may have been high, but my body was tired. I took on the mood of the person working because I didn't protect my own energy. And not only that, but the charity housed its own level of energy too! Places that house old and used "stuff" are heavy with that "old-stuff" energy. What's more, we can take on that dark energy when we are depleted emotionally or physically, even when our spirits are high. So pretty much—I goofed. My boundaries were weak and in need of a tweak.

Here's another example. Say your nephew Jack has just flown in from Alaska, where he has lived for the past seven years. The whole family is excited to see him and meet his soon-to-be fiancé Kerri. However, the second you lay eyes on her you dislike her completely. You are one intuitive-hip person so you consider sharing your insight with your big brother—a.k.a. Jack's dad. If you had poor boundaries you would. If you had decent boundaries you would step back and check in with your higher soul-self to see why you might feel this way. As you check in, you realize that there was no knowing feeling or *aha* moment upon meeting Kerri. After you breathe into that realization, the first thing that pops into your head is a flash of your gymnastics teacher. You hated your gymnastics teacher, and her doppelgänger is standing with your nephew right now! When you stepped back, you ignited your boundaries, leaving your intuition able to help solve what could have been a crime.

Get it? Now that we've identified examples of poor boundaries, let's learn how to give our boundaries the tweak they need!

Tools & Techniques
Bubble Up

Who—Every one of us!
What—Clear your energy and protect your body,
mind, and spirit
When—Anytime
Where—Anywhere

Sit in a comfortable chair with your feet planted firmly on the ground. You may need to place a pillow under your feet to help them touch something solid. Relax your arms. Rest your hands on your thighs—palms facing up if it is comfortable, down if it is not. Take six slow, deep breaths from inside your lower belly, breathing in and out through your nose. Slowly slide your feet (preferably bare, but with socks is okay) back and forth on the ground three times.

- Picture a cord that resembles the root of a huge tree flowing out from the middle of each foot. As the root grows, another buds from the base of your spine and gently attaches to the roots coming from the soles of your feet. The connection looks like an upside-down letter Y.

- Watch the roots fall softly and swiftly to the core of the earth, attaching there. Wrapping around it, the cord makes its way back up to your feet and spine. Consider yourself grounded!

- Now picture a light-filled mist flowing up from the ground and surrounding you in an egg-shaped bubble. Imagine a clear coating forming around it. Nothing but love can penetrate the light—nothing.

- Close your eyes and bring to mind two or three people, on either side of the veil, who love you. Allow yourself to experience how it feels to be loved by them. Inhale the feeling. Allow the energy of their love to swirl around you and through you.

- Inhale and lock in the feeling. Exhale and know that it is available to you at any time. (It makes an excellent companion when you feel misunderstood, picked on, or lonely.)

- Say to yourself, "I am awake to the spirit within, and walk with faith and grace beside me. Within this vibrant space, I am free."

Tools & Techniques
Safe, Centered, and Secure

Who—Every one of us who has ever felt spacey!
What—Centering and grounding through nature
When—When you're alone
Where—Somewhere quiet and near nature

- Listen to yourself breathe for a few minutes. Inhale energy from the earth. As you exhale imagine your breath circling back down to the core of the earth.

- As you slowly breathe in and out through your nose notice how you feel closer and closer to the earth.

- Silently repeat to yourself, "I am loving and I am loved. I am forgiving and I am forgiven. I release and I am released. I am a divine child of the Universe. I am safe, I am loved, and I am valued."

- Imagine energy circling in and around you radiating with white light and filling you with the peaceful flow of the Universe.

- Enjoy nature and walk with the intention of stepping back into yourself.

Tools & Techniques
Ejecting Barbs, Spikes, and the Like

Who—Anyone who has ever felt criticized
What—Neutralize the effects of criticism
When—Anytime you know you will be alone for
five minutes
Where—Your car, home, office, or any private spot

- Grab your cell phone and find a lovely visual of the color magenta. Magenta is associated with harmony, balance, psychic ability, and spiritual development.

- Turn off your ringer and place your cell phone at least twelve inches away from your body.

- Close your eyes, breathe from your core, and imagine a magenta mist coming up from the earth and safely encircling you in an egg-shaped form.

- Picture all the negative thoughts and actions that are pointed your way becoming totally weightless as you inhale deeply through your nose. As you exhale through your mouth, imagine them rapidly springing off you, propelled backward, then dropping down and returning to the earth to be cleared and cleaned.

- Now picture all the negative thoughts and actions you intentionally or unintentionally aimed at others (or yourself!) popping rapidly off as you exhale through your mouth.

- Inhale and exhale deeply and slowly through your nose and give thanks for the light in and around you as the magenta mist turns an iridescent white.

- Say, "I shine my light on every dark thought that arises. They turn into whispers with wings that fly away. I am filled with a quiet peace and am now in my now."

Tools & Techniques
Boundaries in a Bottle

Who—Anyone who could use a quick boundary fix
What—Expeditiously clear the energy in and around you
When—When you wish to clear your mind or you feel like your boundaries are askew
Where—Any private or semi-private space

- Fill a small clean glass spray bottle with purified water. Add several drops of sage essential oil or salt (either sea salt or kosher salt).

- Imagine that you are surrounded by a white light.

- Stand in the middle of the room and spray the air above your head three times.

- Close your eyes and touch the tip of your middle finger to the top of your thumb. This is known as the Akash mudra, which helps activate positive thought and strengthens the intuitive voice. Keep your other fingers straight but relaxed.

- Say, "The brilliant light of my soul shines and I feel imbued with confidence, peace, and courage. I am filled with appreciation and am radiant with white light."

You have now bounced yourself back into your intuitive-happy self! Using one of these grounding techniques is a beautiful way to start your day—or clear your energy and protect your body, mind, and spirit. Once you learn how to ground yourself the good will freely flow through you and anything else will fall away!

Chapter 5

Numbers, Symbols, and Signs

Numbers, symbols, and signs
act as my compass.

As I sat down to write *The Happy Medium: Awakening to Your Natural Intuition* around 2007, a strange feeling came over me. Actually, it grabbed hold of me and shook furiously. It wasn't a spirit, though—it was my fear! How on earth was I qualified to write about intuition? Yes, I had twenty-five some years of hard-won experience, but I certainly wasn't Edgar Cayce, or Edward and Holland, my favorite John mediums. What was I thinking, agreeing to write about myself and my work? I prayed for a sign that I was meant to write this book.

It was about midnight, so I took my darling dog Baci outside before I turned in for the night. I saw, to my horror, two sets of glowing eyes hovering at about four feet from my small puppy. I started to dash over to Baci when the eyes bounded away and I realized—the eyes belonged to two deer! Deer were not an overly common sighting in my suburban neighborhood. I took the sighting as a sign, and Baci and I headed for the comfort of bed.

The next morning, after I dropped my sweet five-year-old daughter Sophia off at our synagogue for preschool, I stopped by my favorite coffee place in South Minneapolis before heading into the office. The sun was out, I had my giant vat of coffee, and I was feeling a bit more confident than I had the night before.

I giggled to myself about the deer and saw something bright, big, and yellow out of the corner of my eye. Talk about weird—it was three giant, bright-yellow butterflies and they were flying right at me! The whole thing began to feel even stranger as the butterflies surrounded me and flew in circles a few inches away from my collarbone and circled me seven times. I stood still after they left and thanked G-d for such a beautiful sign!

Minutes later I had almost reached my car when I started to doubt that the deer and butterflies were signs.

(Yes, I can feel that unclear!) I silently asked the butterflies to return, and to my utter and honest amazement, they did, and circled around me yet again. They were messengers from the Universe and I finally got it.

Numbers, symbols, and signs are in our lives for a reason—they are one example of how our guides and loved ones communicate with us through the language of intuition. They help illuminate the messages our higher soul-selves crave. Guides, angels, hunches, and even hugs do the same!

Our guides know us better than anyone, so they tend to be rather potent, and sometimes humorous, in their approach to communication. It's not always easy to decipher their presence because we are completely familiar with their energy, even thinking it is *our own* since they have been with us long before our births and will remain with us beyond death. We always have their support and are never alone.

As I wrote in *The Happy Medium: Awakening to Your Natural Intuition*, we all have one senior, full-time spirit guide that helped us prepare for this life, as well as several transitioning junior guides. They are never critical and are always loving and supportive. When I was young, I referred to my guides as inner-parents, because that is what I thought they were.

How exactly, you may wonder, do your guides reach you, and you them?

One way is through signs, of course! Have you ever had the experience of running into the same friend or acquaintance over and over again? Typically our guides arrange this because seeing them *is* the message, or perhaps they have a message for you and you for them. Take note of your conversation, including how you feel and its overall theme.

Our guides also get our attention by directing a slight tingling sensation to the top of our head and energetically tapping our pineal gland. This gland sits in the central part of our brain that levels with the middle of our eyes and has long been referred to as the "third eye." The philosopher Descartes described the pineal gland as the "principal seat of the soul."

Our guides may also reach us through various modes of communication such as dreams, coincidences, and serendipitous events, and even through the repeating lyrics of a song (don't worry, I'm not implying that they sing!).

Here's an example of one of the varied ways our guides use music to reach us. You walk into a shoe store and, by chance, hear a melody and are moved by the lyrics. The next day you recurrently hear the same song. First it's on your neighbor's stereo, the melody drifting over to your side of the street. An hour later you turn on your car radio and there it is again! So now the question is, what's the message?

Listen to the words of the song and notice how you feel when you do. Your guides want you there. The meaning will bring you to a place of power, not depression. The voice of our intuition is soothing and discerning, never critical or blaming.

Our guides also reach us through words or symbols in books, magazines, and even articles floating across the screens of our computers as we check social media. Be mindful of your dreams, as well—spirits on the other side like to reach us through that medium.

It's not uncommon to try so hard to see, feel, or sense a sign from a loved-one-in-spirit that you actually miss what's right in front of you. Or rather, overlook it. Just remember, there simply is no such thing as a coincidence. You do not have to try too hard to notice a calling card from a crossed-over loved one, just remain open-minded and pragmatic at the same time. (Read more about signs from those who have transitioned to the other side in Chapter 8.)

Signs from the other side are not the only signs to consider. Insightful messages may arrive in innumerable forms. For example, numbers are amazing tools of communication from our higher self, our guides, and the Universal Source. Numerology is the study of numbers, and the mystical manner in which they reflect certain character tendencies. Numbers in sequence especially hold amplified power.

My initial interest in numerology began years ago with the study of mysticism, which quickly became the study of Jewish mysticism and the Kabbalah. The precise translation of the word Kabbalah is "that which is received," from the Hebrew root, Qof-Beit-Lamed. Kabbalah numerology is one of the ancient systems of calculating the effects of numbers in this universe.

Because there are so many variations regarding the meaning and vibration behind each number, I love to scroll through books like *Numerology and the Divine Triangle* by Faith Javane and websites to find a narrative that fits for me. I am still a novice at understanding numerology but I am expert at reading energy. So, as I do with most everything, I read the energy of numbers.

Seeing numbers in double, triple, or quadruple forms intensifies their qualities. When we see them over and over again, it also illustrates that we are in sync with the Universe. My understanding is that the number *one* is said to be the number of action, originality, and creation, the number that started it all. *Two* is associated with cooperation, harmony, and relationship, and *three* is associated with the vibration of creative self-expression, manifestation, and abundance.

The number *four* resonates with the vibration of stability, strength, position, materiality, dependability, and practicality. *Five* resonates with the vibration of high energy, adventure, logic, ethics, and independence. *Six* resonates with harmony, creativity, music, love, family, idealism, and loyalty. The number *seven* vibrates with balance, spirituality, solitude, and truth seeking. *Eight* holds the commanding vibe of inner-strength, personal power, finances, and balance.

The number *nine* resonates with the vibe of amiability and generosity. Since I am listing my understanding of the vibrations associated with numbers one through nine, and I love odd little truths, it is fun to include this interesting fact: if you multiply any number with nine, the outcome reduces to nine. (7 x 9 = 63, and 6 + 3 = 9.)

Though math always terrified me as a child, I find numerology to be fascinating, and as I said, it is a remarkable way for our guides, as well as those in spirit, to communicate with us.

So when we randomly look at the clock and see 11:11 over and over, the number one is amplified. From the perspective of this medium, the meaning behind the double numbers rests, in part, on what we were doing right before the double numbers appeared. Many believe that when we continuously see 11:11 it is a sign that we are waking up, spiritually speaking, to the divine light within and becoming more and more aligned with our soul's purpose. In other words, we are sparkling!

While numbers have long held meaning, another intuitive sign has to with bodily reactions. For example, if I have felt drawn to something for a long while and the subject makes my solar plexus dance and my body buzz I know that it is the right path. The solar plexus, also called the celiac plexus, is a complex network of nerves situated in the abdomen, just above the belly button. It is the energy center associated with personal power, self-discipline, self-esteem, and confidence. A dancing solar plexus is a sign! My language of intuition employs my solar plexus several times a day.

When someone says something that gives you pause, makes you feel warm, and/or results in goose bumps popping up on your arms, it's your intuitive voice saying, *Pay attention to this, it's true!* This can even include randomly spoken words by strangers that just happen to hold relevant messages.

A good rule of thumb is to be open-minded and agree to see things from an enriched perspective. If you have found yourself parking next to new cars for two weeks straight it's not a coincidence, because there is no such thing—there's always a reason for it! It could be that a new car is in your future, or that you will be riding in one soon. Set your intention and ask the Universe to please provide clarification. Keep in mind that the clarification will likely be given by way of a sign!

Signs have always existed. You are now far more fluent in the language of your intuition so can navigate with greater perception. Everything has meaning; just agree to find the highest good in all conditions and the signs will be illuminated.

Feel inspired to take a chance and wonder if you should? Hesitant about the big decision you just made and could use some divine support? Keep seeing double numbers on the clock and have a feeling it symbolizes something? With these awareness tools, learn how you can be inspired and supported by numbers, symbols, and signs!

Tools & Techniques
Triggering Numbers, Symbols, and Signs

Who—Everyone
What—Dial into the meaning of numbers, symbols, and signs that are present in our everyday lives
When—You want support through signs
Where—Anywhere

Stand or sit with spine straight and legs and arms uncrossed. Gently close your eyes and listen to the sound of your breath as you slowly inhale and exhale three times through your nose. Feel the rise of your belly as you take in another breath and relax into yourself as you exhale. As you inhale a fourth time envision a golden-white light moving up from the core of the earth through your feet and out from the top of your head. The golden-white light then encircles your body three times and floats back down to the core of the earth.

If you have a specific question, set your intention and ask the Universe to please provide clarification. Say,

"Universe, please provide an answer to this question: (state question). I am open and receptive."

- Open your eyes and move throughout your day with an awareness of the numbers, symbols, and signs that may be speaking to you.

- We are building our psychic muscle here so remember, acknowledging the small signs is every bit as important as acknowledging the big ones. No sign is too small. If it has meaning, it has meaning.

- The way you feel about the sign is significant. What feels good *is* good. Even if the sign denotes something sad, the emotional heads-up a sign provides is beneficial.

- As you feel yourself react to the sign, notice any pictures that flash through your mind or focal points where the sensation landed in your body.

- If you believe the sign appeared to encourage you to move forward on something but you feel unsettled when you think about it, simply pause. A solid decision is much like a fine red wine—it will feel good as you take it in, and the finish should be spectacular.

- If a sign occurs three or more times, your guides are driving the point home.

- It's a Universal Law that when you ask for help, you will receive it in some form. So ask!

- Some signs that your guides and angels are near include sparkles in the air, flashes of light like fireflies flying by, and a familiar feeling.

- Notice when everything seems to fall quiet and slow down—often it occurs when something *telling* is happening.

- When you have a question for your guides that requires a more detailed answer than *yes* or *no*, head to a pile of books or magazines and pick up the first one you are drawn to. Hold it in your hands, eyes closed, take three deep breaths, and silently ask your question. When the time feels right, open it up and see what is on the page. Certain phrases or words will seem to stand out. They are there to help answer your question.

Our guides and loved ones communicate with us through numbers, symbols, and signs. As we build awareness and open up to our feelings, the meaning will unfold—soon we'll be delighted with how quickly and fluently we speak and understand the language of intuition, transforming signs into signposts that help us navigate with far greater perception.

Chapter 6

Matching Vibe to Vehicle

*My energy is ignited, my thoughts fill me
with light, and the light fills me with joy.*

Recognizing the differences in people's energy is an
amazing and useful intuitive skill. The benefits spill over
into countless other areas, intuitively speaking. When
you are trying to find one of your children in a crowd,
for example, you simply tune into how their energy
feels and walk in the direction of that feeling. As long
as you are a clear conduit—in your super-psychic space,
vibrating at a high speed—this will lead you in the right
direction.

Here's a little exercise to help you tighten up and tone those intuitive muscles. The next time you are at a casual gathering with people you know, but not too well, spend a little time chatting with a number of guests and be aware of how their vibration feels. Does your stomach ache or tingle? Does your heart feel light? Are you overheating or do you feel just right? This is a great way to learn to consciously connect with various types of soul energy and sense the many differences in vibration.

Make your way to the parking lot a few minutes before the event ends and try to match vehicle to guest. Which vehicle shares a similar energy with someone you were talking to at the party?

Tools & Techniques
Car Games

Who—Car lovers and energy buffs
What—Connecting the energy of a vehicle to its owner
When—During a casual gathering at a place with parking
Where—Parking lot

Step into a quiet corner and do this quick breathing exercise. Stand with spine straight and legs and arms uncrossed. Gently close your eyes and listen to the sound of your breath as you slowly inhale and exhale three times through your nose. Feel the rise and fall of your belly as you take another breath and relax into yourself as you exhale. Notice how your body feels as the flow of air moves through you.

Take another deep breath and, as you do, imagine an iridescent white cord, about as thick as the steering wheel in a car, popping out of the middle of each foot and zipping down to the core of the earth where it firmly plugs into its center. As you inhale again, an iridescent white light surrounds your body in an egg-shaped glow. You are now divinely protected and connected to the core of the earth.

You may be drawn to a number of vehicles when you begin this exercise but in order to avoid feeling overwhelmed, choose just two or three. Better yet, let the vehicles choose you!

- Stroll through the parking lot and allow your gaze to be drawn to a vehicle.

- Sink into the feeling you have as you gaze at the vehicle.

- Breathe into the feeling.

- Observe any pictures, names, or sensations that arise as you do.

- Which guest comes to mind (and heart or spirit) when you look at the vehicle?

- Remember where it is parked and, if you wish, find another vehicle and follow the same steps.

- Next head to your vehicle and wait for people to pile out into the parking lot. See who gets into the car or truck you were drawn to.

- No worries if you miss the mark at first—it takes a little practice. Either way, you are pumping up your psychic muscles!

You can play this matching game with many different variations. Just make sure to always release the need to be right and choose to feel peaceful instead. This exercise is about building your psychic muscle and enjoying yourself in the process!

Chapter 7

I Like It, I Love It, I'm Grateful

*Live what you love and
what you love will fill your life.*

Here's a little game to help you lighten and brighten your vibe to a point where you actually feel a natural high. The object is to rapidly find something—anything!—you like, love, or appreciate. As you move through this game, you will find it easier and easier to spot things that make you feel good, and soon you will find things you love around every corner.

Our vibrational frequency is raised through this process—and our vibe is our point of attraction! After applying this technique it is likely that you will intuitively choose the swiftest line at the grocery store, happen upon the least crowded elevator, and find yourself surrounded by people in equally good and appreciative moods.

Playing this game also puts you in a highly perceptive and receptive mode. In this state of being you are magnetic! Watch for serendipitous occurrences to unfold in the shape of answered questions.

Make this game a habit and watch how your intuitive code is decoded and insights become clearer and clearer.

Tools & Techniques
Like Attracts Like

Who—Those who want to get high on their own energy
What—A mood-lifting, energy-buzzing game that creates a natural high
When—Anytime
Where—Throughout the day, every day

Start this exercise by sitting with your spine straight and legs and arms uncrossed. Remember, a straight spine is a tall spine, not a tight spine. Roll your shoulders back and forth once or twice and lift them to your ears and gently drop them back down. Keeping a straight back opens you up spiritually.

Gently close your eyes and listen to the sound of your breath as you slowly inhale and exhale three times through your nose. Feel the rise and fall of your belly as you take another breath and relax into yourself as you exhale. Notice how your body feels as the flow of air moves through you. Take another deep breath, and as you do imagine an iridescent white light filling your lungs and floating sweetly through your entire body. Listen to the soft sound of your breath as you exhale. On the next inhale, say your full name to yourself and notice the sensation of lightness as you exhale.

- Close your eyes and bring to mind your favorite scent. Fill yourself with appreciation for it. Sink into the feeling as you open your eyes.

- As you check out your surroundings, find something you like. What do you see? Say something positive to yourself about whatever it is. Sink into the feeling.

- Now immediately find something else that makes you smile and feel good. Allow the sensation of appreciation to fill you up. Close your eyes and listen to yourself inhale and exhale slowly.

- Open your eyes and spot something else you love. Inhale the feeling. As you exhale allow the sensation of appreciation to fill each cell of your body with light.

- As you find your happy through this technique, just float there! Flashes of insight will abound. Appreciate them and they will multiply.

- Do this for fifteen minutes and feel your whole being shift.

When you think about something and are filled with emotion, you radiate the vibration to the world and the world radiates it back to you. Like attracts like, so how do you *like* that!

Chapter 8

Reaching through the Veil

My love, I haven't left you, I'm here. I am in your heart and I am on the other side of the veil. I laid my hand on your cheek this morning and sat at your feet as you wept last night. You cannot see me as I see you, but you can feel me. Believe it. Our love survived my death and you will survive it also. Live. Dance. Laugh. Love again.

Among the most frequently asked questions I receive are "Are you reading my mind? What am I thinking?" (I'm not because it's truly none of my business.) Another is "What's in my future?" (The answer is whatever is in your mind!) And still another, "Is my deceased mother here? What does she say?" (Loaded question!)

All joking aside, our loved-ones-in-spirit are able to see us, and through their love for us, reach us. And we are able to connect with them through love and the language of intuition.

By now, you have seen firsthand that *The Happy Medium: Speaking the Language of Intuition* is filled with appealing, intuition-boosting practices that have, simply by taking in the information, helped you become more of your intuitive-happy self. So what's happy about death, and why is a chapter about it included in this uplifting book of exercises?

How about this—*death* doesn't really exist. At least not in the finite, *gone forever* way that so many of us have long believed. Death is moving out of the physical form into pure energy, and from one level of consciousness into another. I've heard from many a spirit that it's really like transitioning from one room to the next.

Of course we still deeply feel the loss of our loved ones, usually for the rest of our lives. That's why connecting with someone who has "crossed over"—as in made their transition and gone to heaven—is priceless.

Since your intuition is a natural resource replenished by the love in your spirit and connection to All That Is, it can help you touch the soul of anyone you love, even when they have made their transition to the other side.

Please know we don't call them or try to summon their presence. There's no fancy long-long-distance phone sold to connect with spirits. And if there were, I wouldn't buy it—I'd run the other direction, and fast. I'm not a fan of anything remotely like the Ouija board. What I am a fan of is love.

Remember these three things: Love never dies. Your loved one knows when it is appropriate to visit. And we can, at any time, fill ourselves with love for them and ask for a dream or a sign that they are doing okay.

It's wise to cover yourself, inside and out, with an all-purpose prayer or positive affirmative words before you begin. This means you connect with your love of self and love for your Higher Power. If the words *G-d, Universe, Higher Power*, etc., don't feel right to you, you can always connect with your love of nature.

It is relevant to note that as a medium I see, hear, feel, and smell things, intuitively speaking. I don't hear full sentences from spirits, but I do hear letters, and sometimes even names, although it sounds like someone is talking to me from underwater. Spirits often send emotions and scenes I can see in my head. It's kind of like a spirit code, and the emotional system is the key. Spirits communicate through my own emotional system, and do the same with everyone. Now that you are learning the language of your own intuition, you will be able to comprehend and respond!

This exercise is designed to help you become aware of visits from spirits, and decode messages and signs from the other side.

When we sport our high-flying vibe we are better able to translate these messages and feel the love and light within them! So in this exercise feel your feelings, appreciate what is in and around you, and allow your inner-self to soar.

Tools & Techniques
Soul Calling Card

Who—Those who want to understand more about the other side and connect with a lost loved one

What—Learning to recognize visits and signs from the other side

When—You have seven to twenty-seven minutes alone

Where—A quiet place where you will be undisturbed

On some level we are always connecting with those we love, even when we are not conscious of it. Living our lives as our intuitive-happy selves helps us make that connection. Begin this exercise by dialing into a higher frequency. It's essential that you raise your vibe and step into your intuitive-happy self because it protects you, makes you a better interpreter of the language of your intuition, and lights up your spirit so those who love you can more easily see your light!

Open up to how you feel and then fill yourself with gratitude and light by acknowledging three things you appreciate about this moment.

Next sit with your spine straight, with legs and arms uncrossed. Slowly raise your hands up and reach for the sky. Bring them back down and rub your palms together until you feel them become warm. Now rest your hands on your thighs with palms facing up. Gently close your eyes and listen to the sound of your breath as you slowly inhale and exhale through your nose three times. With each inhale imagine an iridescent, sparkle-filled white light traveling up from the core of the earth and moving through your body, energetically grounding, loving, and protecting you. The sparkle and love grow stronger as you breathe into its heat. Feel how safe and sound you are within this connection.

Remember, spirits communicate through our intuition, and therefore our feelings. It is wise to set the tone appropriately, so recognize that you are about to radiate your love for someone on the other side and that this does not equate to summoning them. Appreciate that love does not die, and that those in spirit always have a sweet awareness of you.

- Picture a scene in your mind of puppies, kittens, or deer playing in a field. How does your heart feel? Is there a bright, popping, and uplifting feeling or a heavy, weighted, and dark feeling?

- If you feel uplifted and bright, notice and hold the feeling. If you feel weighted and dark, delete the scene from your mind and reach for one that makes you delight in nature.

- Next bring to mind any event where you laughed and enjoyed the moment. Notice and hold the feeling.

- Now think of someone you love dearly who is on the other side. Remember, in great detail, how it felt to be in a room with them and be loved by them. Hold the feeling.

- How does your heart feel? Is there a bright, popping, and uplifting feeling? If so, hold the feeling and breathe into it. If not, find a memory of a loved one on the other side that does provoke a light feeling.

- As you hold the feeling, memorize it in detail. This is your loved one's vibration. Think of it as a soul calling card.

- The next time you feel that same loved-up sensation out of the blue, you likely are undergoing a sort of metaphysical text message from that particular loved one. A metaphysical text message is a *Hello, I love you* from a loved one in heaven. It can be delivered through a number of means—consider coins, serendipitous events, or even electrical devices, which are popular conduits used by spirits. For example, cell phone alarms may go off unexpectedly or calls and texts may come in from a number that is similar to your loved one's cell number.

- Think of another person who has made their transition to the other side. Is there a bright, popping, and uplifting feeling? Notice and hold the feeling.

- Note the differences in how you feel when you reflect on both of your loved-ones-in-spirit. Now that you have experienced and held more than one sensation, you will be better able to understand the language spirits use to communicate their presences.

- When you feel these sensations ask yourself if it's an anniversary of their death, a birthday, or some other celebration. Those in spirit often drop by as a way of acknowledging a significant day.

- Metaphysical messages often involve signs that make sense to only loved ones, such as randomly placed coins, butterfly sightings (even during the heart of winter), or frequently spotted license plates with a special loved one's initials.

Tools & Techniques
Clear and Concise

Who—Anyone who wishes to clear their mind to increase the clarity of their insights

What—Learning to clear your mind to increase clarity of insight and tune in to messages from the other side

When—You have eighteen minutes alone

Where—A quiet place where you will be undisturbed

You can use your intuition to interpret why you receive signs from loved ones on the other side, and what they are trying to impart. (If you wish to see a comprehensive list of signs from the other side, *The Happy Medium: Awakening to Your Natural Intuition* has a great one to help build your skill level so you can not only notice, but ascertain what the signs mean.)

If, for example, you have been feeling heavy and sluggish all day with thoughts of a friend who has transitioned to the other side and can't figure out why (and it's not a birthday, anniversary, or a favored time of year) stop and just breathe.

- Imagine that your mind houses a giant white-board with symbols, words, and pictures denoting your thoughts.

- Now visualize yourself cleaning it so it sparkles. Breathe into the feeling of a cleared mind.

- Close your eyes and listen to the sound and hum of each word as you say (out loud or to yourself), "My mind is open, my heart is receptive, and all my insights are now clear and concise."

- Ask your inner-parents (a.k.a. guides) to help clarify why your friend has been on your mind. If you don't receive a picture, symbol, or sign within three minutes, let it go, knowing the answer will be provided at the perfect time.

- You might, for example, recognize the particular aroma of your friend's perfume as it fills your car or the sound of their voice humming to the song playing on your radio, meaning their spirit is very likely saying, "Hello, I'm here to say I love you!"

- Move through your day and take note of reoccurring conversations around you, including advertisements on billboards, TV, and radio—anything that reminds you of your friend. What story is unfolding for you?

- Ask yourself if you are in need of their kind support. When you ask yourself this question, do you feel a bright, popping, and uplifting sensation, or a heavy, weighted, and dark feeling? If you feel light, bright, and uplifted you have (perhaps unconsciously) wished for your friend's support and it has arrived.

This process deepens your knowledge of the language of intuition. Always remember you walk with faith and grace beside you, and are awakening more and more to the spirit within.

Chapter 9

Magnet and Steel

Fill yourself with thoughts that bring you joy
and happiness, and illumination and light
will follow. We are all beings of light, and light
is energy. Everything is energy. Everything.

The thoughts you think, along with your feelings and emotions, control your vibration. Your vibration is a magnet and everything that comes to you is steel.

The people that surround you are those you magnetized your way. And the circumstances you love most— you attracted those as well! True, you may not be conscious about *how* you've done this, but you did it either way.

As Gautama Buddha wrote, "We are what we think. All that we are arises with our thoughts. With our thoughts, we make the world." And Albert Einstein affirmed, "Imagination is everything. It is the preview of life's coming attractions."

The thoughts you think—along with your feelings, the words you speak, and your emotions—control your vibration. Your vibration, or vibrational frequency, is a magnet and the steel is everything you think about, speak about, and feel. It's the Universal Law of Attraction in action.

A great way to approach this is through the eyes of love, especially through the love we feel for our children. All three of my children were taught how to tie their shoes, yet they never wanted to stop running, jumping, and climbing long enough to do so. Once they connected the experience of tripping to their untied laces they became eager to get the job done. During this process I never thought my kids unwise or lazy. They were simply learning about life, just as we are all continuously learning about life.

As you begin to understand the Universal Law of Attraction you are far less likely to trip, and far more likely to receive what you are looking for—or at least what you have been thinking about!

Through gratitude, as well as making choices based on what makes you happy, you strengthen the magnetic pull of your vibrational frequency. When you make a habit out of doing what you love, what you love will begin to fill your life! This raises your vibe, which as you know, causes you to become more intuitively aware.

It's simple: allow your happiness to be at the heart of every decision, and know that your intuition will lead you there. When you move in the direction of what feels good and true, your solar plexus will start to dance.

Remember, the solar plexus, also called the celiac plexus, is a complex network of nerves situated in the abdomen above your belly button. It is the energy center associated with personal power, self-discipline, self-esteem, and confidence. It is linked to the third chakra (one of the seven primary whirling circles of energy throughout the body), and is amazing at signaling what is best for your soul.

There is no need to worry that your quest for doing what feels good will lead you down the path of darkness, because it is only in the light that we feel truly good.

Let's say you and a friend take a trip together and seating on the airplane is super tight. The flight attendants offer to move a few people to first class and you are one of them. You have never flown first class and are surprised when your gut (solar plexus) drops instead of dances at the prospect. First class may sound like fun, but spending time with your friend *feels better*.

You know what you like because you know how you feel. And you do what you like because you like how it feels. Your intuitive voice will become louder and stronger as you continue to move in the direction of what you love!

Here's another way to think about it. Do you remember the old-fashioned pinball machines? The objective is to score as many points as possible and not allow the steel balls to go down the drain. Points are scored when the steel ball bangs into the bell-ringing, light-flashing targets on the field. The game is over when all of the steel balls fall into the drain.

Throughout various stages of my life I have felt like *I am* the metal ball haphazardly banging into different targets. It's a funny visual that my guides drop onto the screen in my head when I *react* to events in my life instead of consciously and deliberately *creating* them.

I demagnetize from feeling like a metal ball by taking a few breaths, connecting to my higher soul-self, and going in the direction of whatever feels good and true. It also helps emotionally unhook and unstick myself from other people's unkind deeds and my own negative thoughts. I then lift up my vibration and become the magnet I'm meant to be!

Tools & Techniques
Unhook and Unstick
to Get Rid of Your Ick

Who—Those who seek more joy and are ready to use their intuition to get there

What—Magnetizing the good through intuition

When—When you have fifteen minutes and wish to attract the good

Where—Your car, home, or office

Sit, stand, or lie down with feet and arms uncrossed. Close your eyes and say your full name. Imagine a sparkling white light moving up from the core of the earth, and a sparkling golden light moving down from the heavens, touching and joining as they move through you. As you inhale slowly through your nose, imagine breathing in the sparkling golden light. As you exhale, imagine the sparkling golden light surrounding you. You are divinely protected.

Your vibe or vibrational frequency is your point of attraction. It's your magnet. So how can you tweak your magnet so that what is steel and drawn to you is delightful and not a downer?

The first way is simple: allow your happiness to be at the heart of every decision, and allow your intuition to lead you there. Here's how.

- When you are faced with a decision, take a deep breath and focus on your solar plexus.

- Ask yourself what feels good and true, and think of your choices one at a time.

- Is your gut dancing or dropping in answer?

- Dancing means move toward or forward.

- Dropping means pause and step back.

- It is always wise to employ your heart, gut, and head. So follow your heart, trust your gut, and use your head.

- As we learned in Chapter 3, if your heart, gut, and head are all saying *yes* in unison, chances are really fabulous that you are moving in the right direction.

- Visualize a giant magnet hovering safely and securely above your head. Imagine inhaling golden-white light, and as you exhale, the magnet pulls out unwholesome self-doubt and replaces the space with pure white light.

The second technique is about your thoughts. I don't believe that we are in complete control over every thought that runs through our heads but we *can* control what we do with them. We can either focus on them or not. That is our choice, and the results are powerful.

- Since whatever we focus on grows, choose to focus on thoughts that feel good, empowering, and positive to think about.

- Focus on something you are grateful for and inhale the feeling. Find your happy, memorize the feeling, and float there. Your pattern of thought is something like muscle memory. Continuously flex these good thoughts and feelings.

- If you repeatedly have a heavy thought, pull your attention away from it and replace it with something, anything brighter.

- If a particularly stubborn critical thought runs incessantly through your head, move your attention to your breathing or to affirmative thoughts such as:

  ° "My energy is ignited, my thoughts fill me with light, and the light fills me with joy."

  ° "As I fill my lungs with clean white light I allow my thoughts to shift. I now recognize who I am and honor my wishes, wants, and desires."

- ° "My thoughts now find tranquility and rest in an ever-increasing stream of harmony."

- ° See Chapter 13 for more affirmations.

- This process realigns you with thoughts that are filled with light.

- Imagine a giant white magnet hovering safely and securely above your head. Envision inhaling golden-white light. As you exhale, the magnet pulls out all old, worn-out thoughts and replaces them with clean fresh air and white light.

The third technique is about feelings and emotions. Feelings and emotions drive your vibe. So how can we *have them* and *not be had by them?*

- Your feelings are a gift from the Universe. What you do with them is your gift back. Feelings are the gateway to your intuition and it is wise to respect them.

- Your feelings are like beautiful children. Compassionately listen to what they have to say. There is no need to fall into them. Just allow them the floor, so to speak, until they feel heard. Then move on and move through.

- Emotions are the story you tell yourself about what your feelings mean, so your emotional response is always in reaction to your feelings. If you find yourself caught in your emotions, which is not uncommon, go back to the original feeling from whence they came! Hug the feeling and allow the sensation to move through you.

- Imagine a giant white magnet hovering securely and safely over your head. Inhale golden-white light, and as you exhale imagine all of the old, over-used emotional reactions steadfastly drawn out by the magnet, leaving a peaceful, quiet space in their wake.

- Old feelings and emotions are based on the very moment they occur. Remember that your moment has now changed. This perspective alters your point of attraction from fear to acceptance and love.

- Move through your days with a feeling of appreciation and always reach for what you love.

- See the huge magnet hover steadily and safely above your head. Squeeze your eyes tight for three seconds and feel a slight tugging sensation in your forehead, chest, and stomach as all thoughts and memories that do not serve your higher soul-self are pulled out by the magnet. Envision the magnet floating away and a peaceful, confident feeling washing over you.

- Breathe into feeling. Allow yourself to float in the moment and inhale the light. Feel the energy of gratitude fill you up, mind, body, and spirit.

- Agree that, for one week, you will allow your happiness to be at the heart of every decision and you will allow your intuition to lead you there. Agree that, for one week, you will choose not to indulge in negative thoughts or words, and you will turn your thoughts to the positive.

- At the end of the week, ask yourself if you feel happier and more insightful. If your solar plexus dances, make it a lifelong habit! If your solar plexus don't dance, it's okay! You are establishing a new way of moving through your life, and it can take time. Start with step one and repeat!

Tools & Techniques
The Flow of Good Decisions

Who—Those who seek more joy and are ready to use their intuition to get there

What—Magnetizing the good through moving in the direction of what makes you happy

When—When you have fifteen minutes and wish to attract the good

Where—Anywhere you are able to quiet your mind and sit undisturbed

Sit in a chair with your spine straight and legs uncrossed. Bring to mind the sound of waves in the ocean. Imagine sitting comfortably on a beach and watching the water move. Breathe into the scene and slowly move back and forth with the water. Gently inhale and exhale through your nose, filling your lungs completely and then exhaling the air fully.

- Continue to breathe and imagine waves. As you inhale, move back. As you exhale, move forward.

- Continue this motion slowly, and bring to mind a recent time you made a decision.

- Go back in your mind and feel your body. Was your solar plexus dancing or dropping?

- When you make a decision that is good for you, you know your intuition is giving you a thumbs up because your solar plexus dances and you feel good. When you make a decision that is not good for you, you know your intuition is giving you a thumbs down because your solar plexus feels as though it has dropped.

- Agree that for the next seventy-two hours you will practice going in the direction of what makes you happy and feels good and true, even if means you have to suspend your people-pleasing side.

Your intuition is the voice of your soul. You can reach your soul by attuning yourself to what you want and manifesting it. Remember your vibration is not about who you are, it is how you are. Tweak your magnetism by filling yourself up with thoughts that bring you joy, gratitude, and happiness, and the light will follow!

Chapter 10

Intuitive Shopping

Every second of your life is divinely kissed.

I've never been a huge fan of shopping. Don't get me wrong, I love wearing fun clothes and eating healthy foods. But shopping for them, not so much. When I'm in the right space, though, it's a breeze—I set my intention and often walk right to what I'm shopping for. My intuition acts like my own personal shopper and takes the monotony out of the experience! Yours can as well and here's how.

The goal is to align your vibration with the product you wish to purchase. This way it will be easier to find, and you may even notice it finds you. That is, if it is for your higher good. That is the one essential condition to using your intuition—it must be used for the greater good. If it is used for anything less, even if you hit your target, you will be shooting blanks.

In this exercise, let's let our intuition guide us to our shopping goal. Let's say you're heading to the mall to find a dress or suit for a party. You are not big on shopping and within an hour your brain usually becomes fuzzy, so time is of the essence. Or maybe you love shopping but need something in particular and don't know where to start. Lead with your intuition and the results will make you want to dance!

Tools & Techniques
Activating Your Own Personal Shopper from Within

Who—Anyone who could use a little help from their intuition with shopping

What—Letting intuition act as a personal shopper and help you locate the goods, fast

When—You want help buying a special something for yourself or someone else

Where—Large shopping malls and grocery stores

Ignite your light and dial into a higher frequency by sitting or standing with legs and arms uncrossed and spine straight. Gently close your eyes and listen to the sound of your breath as you slowly inhale and exhale three times through your nose. Feel the rise and fall of your belly as you breathe, and relax into the flow of air as it moves through you. Say your full name to yourself. As you inhale fully, bring to mind something you appreciate about this day, and as you exhale feel your breath as it gently exits through your nose. Inhale, filling your lungs completely, and bring to mind something you appreciate about yourself, being present with your breath as you exhale.

Imagine sitting by the ocean, listening to the waves as they dance, in answer to the ocean tides. Feel yourself sway back and forth with the sound. Enjoy the freedom of the motion.

Give thanks that you are aware of how you feel. Experience the energy of gratitude and the happiness it brings. This flips the consciousness switch—your intuition is now in the *on* position. Psychic shopping can now begin!

- Dial into your intuition by setting your intention before you leave for the mall. Say, for example, you intend to find a fabulous, affordable outfit for a semiformal event.

- Picture the general look you are going for. Imagine the colors you love, and the feel of fabric you prefer.

- Visualize yourself finding a fabulous suit or dress in your size. Envision how it would feel to wear it at the event. Does the picture in your mind *feel* good? If not, find a picture that does!

- When you arrive at your shopping destination, take three slow deep breaths and bring to mind the feel of the ocean tides. Feel the pull of the water as it responds to the gravitational forces of the sun and moon. When your personal shopper is at hand, that is how you will feel directed—as if by a tide in the ocean.

- Imagine feeling gently tugged in the direction of the garment you seek. This may feel like a little nudge or just that you "want" to go in a certain direction for some yet unknown reason. Follow this feeling!

- Be fluid in your thinking. For example, if you happen upon a beautiful blouse or shirt in the right color and slick black pants that you cannot put down, this could still be the outfit for you. Or if your budget calls for a dress or shirt that is around or under $100 and you find something you love for $105, be flexible and buy it. Remember, it is the *feel* of the outfit you are magnetizing your way.

Now let's say you are at a mall shopping for an outfit for a special occasion you are soon to attend. You find just the right one but it is a size too small.

- Hold the item in your hands and notice in detail what you love about it. Is it the color, the fabric, the style?

- Look at it closely and imagine finding your size. Envision how it would feel to wear it at the event. Does the picture in your mind feel good? If the garment is right, the positive feelings you have for it fastens it to you, energetically speaking. If it doesn't feel good, the outfit may not be the one for you. No worries, you are not alone—your psychic shopper, a.k.a. your intuition, has been ignited.

- Imagine that the garment in your size (or its equivalent) is in the mall and that your inner personal shopper is leading you to it. Envision a tiny silver thread leading you, pulling you in its direction. Go where it leads you!

This technique also works when shopping for a gift for someone else. It works best if you love or at least have genuine affection for the one receiving the gift.

- Envision the face of whoever is going to receive the gift. Recall how it feels to be around this person. Feel your love and/or affection for them.

- Inhale and exhale slowly through your nose while listening to the sound of your breath. Now simply head in the direction you feel compelled to go.

- You may see a shop that seems to glow or have a bright quality of light and color to it. That is your personal shopper at work, so head there.

- Our intuitive voice is heard through our senses and feelings. If the noise level around you drops and everything feels still all of a sudden, you're being called to consciousness. Note your surroundings and allow your body to move you in a certain direction.

- Be open to what you find. You may not be sure why you are drawn to a certain object but be open; it might end up being the perfect gift for them! You are seeking the feeling of happiness it will bring, so if you find something that is not exactly what you had in mind, but it feels right, buy it!

Take stock of how you feel throughout this process and give yourself some metaphysical love by dialing into the higher frequency of appreciation. Your intuitive voice can't help but sing when greeted with appreciation and love.

Chapter 11

Intuition as Matchmaker

Love is the fingerprint of the soul. Leave your fingerprints everywhere.

Everyone has enjoyed watching a good love story (even if the last time we did, it was a cartoon and we were seven years old). The fact is that movies about love sell because everything in the Universe revolves around—you guessed it—love.

Speaking of movies, think of your mind as a projector, and the screen as your life—or rather, the *circumstances* of your life. We all project our thoughts. The energy of this creates the circumstances that unfold every day.

Your energy is the same thing as your vibration. And every thought you think, every word you say, and every feeling you have is projected out and magnetized back. Every single thing that happens to us is a mirror reflection of how we feel, think, and speak—this is big time law-of-attraction stuff. For example, if you are running into nothing but the friendliest of people it is because *you* are radiating a friendly vibe, you magnet you!

So how can we put it into action, and what does it have to do with love and intuition?

Techniques like "What We See Is What We Get" and "Like Attracts Like" raise our vibrations and make us a clearer conduits for receiving signs and interpreting the language of our intuition. When we are tuned into our intuition we can act on positive impulses and knowing feelings, and *that* is when all that good stuff will be reflected back to us.

With this in mind, we can essentially hire our knowing soul-self as our matchmaker. The law of attraction is always in action, and through our intuition, we can translate the prompts—left here, right there, cute guy straight ahead (our intuition makes for a great navigator!).

In love, one way to interpret the cues of your intuition is listening to how your solar plexus feels. Remember, a dancing solar plexus means you are in the right place at the right time, compared to when something isn't good for you and your solar plexus feels like it's tanked. It either drops or dances, so pay attention and stay focused because this is the language of intuition.

When you are drawn to someone and feel solid when you are with that person, even though your heart is fluttering wildly and your solar plexus is doing the samba, your knowing soul-self is speaking to you through the language of your intuition and saying *advance*. Be sure to memorize how you feel when something is good and stays good. You want more of that!

Another way to intuitively use the law of attraction in matters of love is by spending time around what you want. Since like attracts like, when I was single I made sure to spend time with the kind of men I wanted to magnetize. In my case, it was my cousins, Ernie and David. They were good of heart and fun to be around, and spending time with them triggered my confidence and happiness, and in doing so, raised my vibrational frequency. To entrain means to connect with, dial into, and draw near, and that is just what I was doing with my high vibrational frequency—drawing in someone with a matching vibe. My intuition led me in the right direction, and yours can do the same!

Tools & Techniques
Trigger and Entrain

Who—Those with a kind and open heart who are
ready to date
What—Dialing into what you love
When—You have ten or fifteen minutes alone
Where—Any place you will be undisturbed

Place your hands on your belly and deeply inhale and exhale
through your nose. Turn your attention to the sound of your
breath and the feel of your belly as it rises and falls. Imagine
a soft pink light radiating out from your heart and slowly
surrounding your whole body. Breathe into the warmth of
the light and absorb the feeling of love and peace it brings.

- First, we clean house. Imagine small, shiny green
  shears floating a few inches away from you. The
  job of the shears is to cut any ties, or etheric
  cords, that are connected to you.

- Etheric cords are energetic threads that are
  activated when we are in a relationship with

someone. As we age and mature, we find that many old relationships are no longer what we want or need them to be. We may have physically walked away, but remember, everything is energy. Cord cutting allows the energetic thread to be severed. This technique breaks the antiquated way of interacting with someone from our past, but doesn't cut us off from love—it just keeps us from getting drained, or from draining anyone else through old obsessive thoughts or ancient emotional patterns.

- Now inhale through your nose and imagine those shiny green shears opening up, and as you exhale, picture them slicing and detaching the cord at base of your spine.

- Inhale gratitude and exhale light.

- Sit with your back straight and legs and arms uncrossed. Remember to keep your spine tall without forcing it. Read each question listed below and close your eyes before responding. If you choose, grab a pen and paper to record your answers. Allow your intuition to show you pictures, send you aromas, and guide you through. This is you speaking the language of intuition.

The questions below will evoke the wonderful vibration of self-love. Love of self is an especially dynamic vibration to radiate when we wish to magnetize someone who will love and appreciate us also.

- ° What are three of my favorite things to do?

- ° What perfume, cologne, or soap do I love to use?

- ° What texture of clothing feels good to wear?

- ° What is my favorite food?

- ° What makes me laugh?

- ° What kind of action or behavior do I find most kind?

- ° What makes a best friend, best?

- Now take a deep breath, and ask for some guidance in answering the following questions.

  - ° What three people make me laugh unselfconsciously?

  - ° Who do I feel most relaxed with?

  - ° Who of my friends have character traits that are similar to those of someone I would like to date?

° Resolve to spend time around friends whose character traits are similar to those of someone you would like around you, as in a partner.

° Now do some of the things you love most! Use your favorite soap, eat delicious food, wear treasured garments, and laugh every chance you get!

Tools & Techniques
Be Who You Want to Be With

Who—You, if you are ready to love honestly through love of self

What—Observing human qualities you love

When—Any week you want to love yourself like you know you deserve

Where—Everywhere

Self-acceptance is self-love in action. Be your own sweetie by being kind, fair, and loving toward yourself. This dials you into magnetizing the energy you seek.

- If you want a significant other to buy you flowers, buy yourself flowers! If you want them to antique shop with you, go antiquing, and if you want them to enjoy car shows, head to a car show and admire both the cars and the people enjoying the show together.

- Think about the qualities you want in a partner and actively embody those qualities yourself. As the week progresses, notice how those same characteristics begin to show up in those around you. *Keep noticing.*

- You will begin to feel guided toward people who are filled with your kind of light. Pay attention to how this feels and move in the direction of that flow.

- Acknowledge that you are open-minded and have an open and loving heart.

Tools & Techniques
Be Present, Be You

Who—You when you are spending time with a love interest
What—Dating pointers
When—You are on a date
Where—Anywhere

- When you meet someone of interest, be mindful of feeling a gravitational pull toward them. If this occurs, and the sensation makes you happy, it is the language of your intuition saying *remain observant and by all means, learn more about this person!*

- If you are having fun and unexpectedly your date says or does something that reminds you of your ex, and not in a good way, check in with yourself. Do you feel resentment? If so, you have some emotional baggage to check. If not, your date *may* share some similar qualities or quirks with your ex, but this person is not your ex so keep your mind open and your heart receptive.

- If you find yourself feeling nervous, as you inhale, picture yourself pulling in white light, and as you exhale imagine your breath falling to the core of the earth and the earth sending up a hug. This will keep you present and in the moment so you can let your shine, shine!

- When you find yourself at ease, give your higher soul-self a wink.

Enjoy each minute—in fact, hug each one as a way of showing gratitude. Delight in the process! As you relax into the moment, know that the energy circling in and around you radiates with white light and fills you with the peaceful flow of the Universe within. Just be yourself— you are not only loved, you are love.

Chapter 12

Getting Stones

*I hug my knowing soul and am awakened
to the spirit within.*

When I was nine years old I had a small assortment of
rocks from around my neighborhood. Not every rock
would make it into my collection—I only chose the ones
I thought were cool and felt good to hold. I would take
a handful of them, lie down, and place them at certain
points around my body. I didn't know why I had the im-
pulse to do this but I always felt more solid afterward. Fast
forward a few decades, and now rocks, crystals, and pre-
cious stones are a part of my spiritual practice.

Gemstones, crystals, minerals, and rocks speak to us through the language of intuition. For the purpose of ease, I will refer to them as gemstones or stones. Feeling drawn to a certain stone means there is something about its mineral composition and structure that is pleasing to your mind, body, and/or spirit. When you see one you love, tune in to where on your body you feel the magnetic pull. This will help you identify where the need for kindness resides. If you pick up a bluish stone, for instance, and you feel a pull in the area of your neck, your thyroid may need some love. Gemstones, crystals, minerals, and rocks are all grounding—they help connect us to the core of the earth, and many believe they have healing properties as well.

Popular gemstones include garnet for its protective energy, hematite for transforming negative energy, carnelian to enhance psychic abilities, and quartz to balance and energize. Two of my personal favorites are amethyst and citrine. Amethyst is sweetly calming and highly perception (intuition) heightening. Citrine is a happy stone that helps with confidence and the digestion of food (and change!). It's one of the only minerals that does not hold negative energy—it is self-cleaning!

I've found that wearing stones alters my energy, which adjusts my vibe and changes what I think and say.

The end result is *I love what I get even if I don't get exactly what I want.* It's that cause-and-effect dance, and certain stones move me in the right direction.

If you are just starting your collection and wish to purchase just a few gems, pick up eight clear quartz stones of equal, or nearly equal, size and shape. Clear quartz is an amplifier of intention and has gained mass popularity over the past few decades for its usefulness. Depending on size, stones are often available for less than a dollar apiece and can do wonders to help balance energy. If you find yourself drawn to carnelian or amethyst, they can also easily be added to the exercise.

However, you don't need to buy gemstones to feel the effects. Rocks you can find on any ordinary walk work beautifully—allow the rocks to choose you! Their energy will draw you in and you will feel it through your heart, head, or gut.

It is important to understand that, though stones are an ancient medium of healing, they should in no way be used as a substitute for proper medical care. There are some outstanding books about stones such as, *Love Is in the Earth: A Kaleidoscope of Crystals* by Melody and *The Crystal Bible* by Judy Hall.

Our soul is a spark that is connected to One Universal Light, and light is energy! As I wrote in *The Happy Medium:*

Awakening to Your Natural Intuition, "Everything in the Universe—clothing, cars, animals, plants, and people— are made of pure energy. Energy itself is made up of atoms. Those who are well versed in science might indicate that energy is neither created nor destroyed, but transformed." The healing and intuitive arts are all about creating positive energetic transformation, and this exercise utilizes stones to do so. Set your intention to strengthen your level of self-love and protection and to open to a new level of psychic awareness.

Just holding certain stones feels amazing, so imagine what it would be like to be surrounded by them! Creating a circle of stones is basically placing crystals around an area to protect, clear, charge, and enhance the space or person. It is also known as gridding. There are an untold number of grid layouts and some are exceedingly complicated. My maxim is "simple is sweet," so grab your stones and let's get started!

Tools & Techniques
Feeling Stones

Who—Those who wish to fortify their boundaries and heighten psychic abilities

What—Raising vibration and intuitive awareness through the ancient use of stones

When—You have an hour or more with no interruptions

Where—A trusted and loved space such as your home

Pick eight clean rocks that are from your garden, acquired on a walk or other travels, or simply eight clean clear quartz stones. Gently close your eyes and listen to the sound of your breath as you inhale and exhale slowly three times through your nose. Feel the rise and fall of your belly as you take another breath and relax into yourself as you exhale. Notice how your body feels as the flow of air moves through you.

Next take three deep breaths—in through your nose, and out through your mouth. Visualize the roots of a giant tree gently wrapping around your ankles and linking you to the earth. Feel how safe and loved you are within this connection. Now open your eyes.

- Hold the stones in your hands. This is a powerful time to ask for guidance. Know that it will be provided through animals, humans, or coincidences.

- Say your intention out loud to influence your heart, soul, and mind. For example: "My intention is to raise my vibration and intuitive awareness through the ancient use of stones."

- Lie face-up with arms and legs uncrossed. Feel the comforting presence of the tree roots around your ankles as you wiggle your toes.

- Place the first stone about two inches from the top of your head with the tip or point directed toward you.

- Moving clockwise around your body, place the second stone two inches from your mid-shoulder area, with the point directed toward your body.

- Next place the third stone two inches from your hip, the fourth stone two inches from your knee, and the fifth stone between the middle of your feet, about two inches away from them both. Repeat the process on the other side of your body.

- You have the option of placing another stone—like a gray garden stone, amethyst, or carnelian—between your brows to enhance the effects of the exercise.

- With eyes closed, stay loose and still for fifteen or twenty minutes within your circle of stones and allow the energy of the Universe to move through the stones and into your body.

- Imagine a fresh, crystal-filled breeze clearing all blocks and moving stagnant, stale energy out through the stones. Feel the cool, clear breeze circling through the rocks and pausing at the soft spot on your head, throat, stomach, heart, base of your spine, and soles of your feet.

- Allow your mind to fill with gratitude for the sweetness in your energy, and know that it is now amplified. Imagine seeing the answers to your questions unfold throughout the next few days.

- Be open to however the answers arrive and know with a deep inner certainty that your questions will be addressed.

- Take three deep inhales and exhales through your nose. Slowly open your eyes and sit up. With gratitude, place your stones into a bowl of clean, tepid water mixed with one teaspoon of kosher salt or sea salt to clean them.

Tools & Techniques
Everybody Must Get Stones

Who—Those who want to feel the warm embrace
of Mother Earth
What—Emulating the energy of stones
When—You want to feel hugged and loved
Where—A trusted space, either indoors or outdoors

- Pick three clean small rocks from your garden
  or that you acquired on a walk. Hold the stones
  in your hands. Bring them to your heart, close
  your eyes, feel your love for the earth, and listen to the sound of your breath as you slowly inhale and exhale three times through your
  nose.

- Lie on your back with arms and legs uncrossed.

- Close your eyes and visualize a giant tree standing lovingly behind you, its roots gently wrapping around your ankles and linking you to
  Mother Earth.

- Lay one stone between your brows. This is your sixth chakra, or your third-eye chakra. In Sanskrit it is known as *Anja*, which means command.

- Lay the second stone at the center of your chest. This is the fourth chakra, the heart chakra, and it's where the physical and spiritual meet. In Sanskrit it is known as *Anahata*, which means unstruck or unhurt.

- Place the third stone on your solar plexus, or third chakra, located right above your belly button. It is known as *Manipura* in Sanskrit, and is associated with clarity and wisdom, as well as seeing inner and outer worlds.

- Breathe in strength and energy from the stones. Feel the weight of the stones and the gift of the lucidity and calm they provide.

- Take three deep inhales and exhales through your nose. Slowly open your eyes and sit up. With gratitude, place your stones into a bowl of clean, tepid water mixed with one teaspoon of kosher salt or sea salt to clean them.

When we work with stones our energy flows into them and the energy of the stones flows into us. The beautiful thing is when we begin to vibrate in a similar way as the stones and are filled with a *quiet peace.* We just have to remember the experience for the calm to remain, though the stones may not.

Chapter 13

The Art of Affirmations

What doesn't work for us doesn't belong with us. Learning to let go is an art—be an artist!

Some people like to doodle or color, but when my pen hits paper I love to write. I adore writing words that inspire and can warmly curl around a wounded heart and add light to the healing process. (I guess I'm a bit of a poet.) When poetry meets intuition, affirmations are born. Imagine my complete delight when I tried my hand at writing my own affirmations and they worked!

Affirmations are constructive, optimistic statements written in the present tense. They are repeated with passion to electrify and impress the subconscious mind. They describe a desired situation and trigger it into positive action.

Basically they help quiet that pervasive internal voice that says *you can't, you won't, and you aren't good enough*! When we turn the thoughts we think and the words we say about ourselves in a positive direction we are affirming our worth and fundamentally creating the goodness in our lives!

Intuition and affirmations act as a team to defragment a cluttered mind. Intuition is a partner in the creative force that magnetizes that which we most desire. Affirmations, also a partner in the creative force, are an instrument of transformation. An affirmation is a proclamation, a declaration of change!

Affirmations eliminate excess noise so we're better able to notice signs and boost intuition and problem-solving skills. They are empowering, and help us rewire fearful thinking.

Here's how they work. If you have trouble saying no to a pushy friend, that nagging voice in the back of your mind might be saying *you can't say no to him, he's bigger than you!*

This is when you say something affirmative about yourself, to yourself. For example, you might say, "I respond to everyone with compassion, even when I have to say no." Do this often enough, and chances are having the courage to say no will no longer be a problem.

Affirmations are not one-size-fits-all. Choose the ones that feel true or simply good to read. You must believe what you are reading, if even just a bit.

If you think all of this is a little sappy, spend a bit of time just listening to what you say to yourself—after listening to the little critic inside your head, you'll likely be willing to give affirmations a try. Remember, what we see, say, and think is what we get. So changing our words changes our minds. Changing our minds alters our energy, and that is what changes our lives.

Tools & Techniques
Affirmations Generate Transformation

Who—Everyone who is aware of the little critic inside their brains

What—Shifting internal messages to create better external circumstances

When—Everywhere

Where—Anywhere

Gently close your eyes and listen to the sound of your breath as you slowly inhale and exhale three times through your nose. Feel the rise of your belly as you take another breath and relax into yourself as you exhale. Now imagine an iridescent white light moving up from the core of the earth and an indigo light moving down from the heavens, touching and joining as they move through you. As you inhale slowly through your nose, imagine breathing in the iridescent white light and as you exhale, imagine the indigo light surrounding you.

Your brilliant, beautiful, all-knowing soul set you here for a reason. The reason is to love and shine. So delight in your own sparkle and ignite the light everywhere. Here's a great way to start.

Have some positive affirmations at hand, such as the ones provided in this book, and check out authors such as Marianne Williamson, Louise Hay, and the late Florence Scovel Shinn for more.

Here are a few ways to weave affirmations into your day. Nibble on a few of them morning, noon, and night and feel your energy swirl and change as the light of your affirmative thinking takes the stage.

- Read a few positive affirmations for three minutes or more right before you close your eyes to sleep.

- Place your affirmations near your bed so you can read one or two upon awakening.

- Print a few affirmations and tape one that makes you smile on your bathroom mirror. Look in your mirror and say an affirmation out loud such as, "I am the perfect me, living out the life I need. I am energized and restored by the light within."

- Tape a favored affirmation to your steering wheel as a reminder to say it out loud every single time you get in your car!

- Choose a favorite affirmation and say it over and over to yourself throughout the day.

- Write your own affirmations!

Affirmations

I am a grateful, willing spirit with a balanced mind and an open heart.

I have within me all that I need. I am love and light in action.

I hug my knowing soul and am awakened to the spirit within.

I choose to change the story I tell about myself—I create my happy ending by creating a happy now.

I feel empowered by my own sense of joy.

I think big, I love big, and I feel big. It is safe for me to be who I am and ask for what I want.

Self-acceptance is self-love in action. I now release the need to be right and feel peaceful instead.

Splendid synchronistic events happen for me every day, powering my transformation. I am filled with the exhilaration of faith, grace, and gratitude.

I am the artist in my life. I now choose to paint, draw, write, and think love and abundance into my world.

I honor my inner voice and am pleased with the outcome. Every decision I make is for my greater good. I now move forward with grace and confidence knowing that the Universe has my back.

I am the perfect me, living out the life I need. I am energized and restored by the light within. My inner doubts no longer run me. I feel confident and am capable, and it shows.

I am my own best ally. I am willing to stand by myself and love myself through every moment of my life, past and present. The light of my being is now infused with incredible tranquility and I am filled with gratitude and grace.

By reciting words that lift me up and fill me with light I turn the ugly verses playing in the back of my mind into beautiful lyrics.

I shine my light on every dark thought that arises and they turn into whispers with wings that fly away. I am filled with a quiet peace and am now in my now.

I happily release old, worn-out thoughts. Letting go facilitates the evolution of the soul.

I greet the words and deeds of others with acceptance and grace.

It all started when I looked for the light. It became stronger when I felt the light from within. Now I see light wherever I go.

It is from a place of calm acceptance that I now recognize the magnificent spark of the soul, mine as well as yours.

I am my own hero. I now believe in the power of my soul and in the power of self-acceptance. I am a living, breathing work of art. I now find grace-filled acceptance in every corner of my life.

In the silence of knowing I fill myself with light. I now laugh my full laugh and dance my full dance.

I let my soul light shine and my intuitive voice sing, and now I am hooked on feeling good.

I feel the rich sensation of silence and the brilliance of the moment. I recognize my soul's desires and am filled with knowing as I move into my ordinary day with extraordinary grace.

Conclusion

*Connect with your knowing soul-self and take
your happy with you wherever you go.*

The language of intuition is *your* language. May you use it to
successfully flow through life and live in a place of abundance,
acceptance, and soul. You truly are pure, love-filled energy.

Remember, the thoughts you think, along with
your feelings and emotions, control your vibration. Your
vibration is a magnet and everything that comes to you is
steel. So changing your words changes your mind, changing your mind alters your energy, and that is what changes
your life! The process naturally makes you more joyful and
far more fluent in the language of intuition.

Make a practice of using the intuition-building exercises in this little book and allow them to assist you in pulling yourself out of a bad mood, dropping you into the perfect outfit, and helping you feel how alive your connection is with those who have transitioned to the other side.

Our feelings are the wings of our intuition. Embrace yours.

As for me, I have danced with my shadows until they became part of my light. Like you, I am many things—powerful, insecure, doubtful, loving, and bold. I am driven, creative, and kind. Though I feel things every bit as deeply as I once did, I am no longer carried away by the depth of my emotions. I have found peace and myself in the happy medium. May you always find your intuitive voice, and may the language of your intuition sing.

Tools & Techniques

Untest

Consider me your "spirited" guide for the final chapter of *The Happy Medium: Speaking the Language of Intuition*. Remember, this is a not-so-final exam because nothing is ever final and it is not a test because there is no way to fail. We all pass!

Please choose the best answer or answers!

1. Before you begin intuitive work of any kind, it's important to . . .

a. Change your socks—spirits hate stinky feet.

b. Think dark thoughts, eat dark chocolate, and sit in a dark room.

c. Dial into a higher frequency by opening up to how you feel, and fill yourself with gratitude and light.

(Answer is C.)

2. "What we see is what we get" refers to . . .

a. When we see and focus on the good, we have more of it.

b. Last call at a bar.

c. Whatever we see, we can take. It's a finders-keepers, losers-weepers thing.

(Answer is A.)

3. You know you are psychic because . . .

A. You love crystal jewelry and look darn good in it.

B. You are excellent at card games such as Old Maid and Go Fish, so you think you will be a natural at reading tarot cards.

C. Everyone is psychic . . . everyone.

(Answer is C.)

4. If your feelings are the wings of your intuition, what is indigestion?

A. Your guide's way of boogying.

B. Discomfort in your abdomen.

C. Bubbles everywhere, magical bubbles.

(Answer is B.)

5. A sign from the Universe that you are insightful and are correct is . . .

A. Goose bumps (also known as angel kisses).

B. Burping, lots of burping.

C. Your solar plexus dancing.

(Answer is A and C.)

6. The chapter about your own personal shopper introduces . . .

A. Astral projection.

B. How to creep on someone at a mall to see what they are buying.

C. How your intuition acts like your own personal shopper.

(Answer is C.)

7. You know you are sensing spirit energy from the other side because . . .

A. The Psychic Network calls you for answers.

B. Your great-aunt Esther keeps coming to mind and the scent of her famous orange chicken has been everywhere all day. You later realize that it is the anniversary of her death.

C. You keep hearing a knock, knock, knock on heaven's door.

(Answer is B.)

8. Your guides are available . . .

A. At Walmart. Grab a six-pack.

B. Nine to five—banker's hours, baby.

C. Always.

(Answer is C.)

9. If you wish to raise your vibration to increase happiness, joy, and insights, what are a few solid things you can do?

A. Practice feeling grateful. Notice everything good that is happening in and around your life. Keep noticing.

B. Pay attention to how you feel. This means how you feel psychically, as well as emotionally. If you feel off or down, do something sweet for yourself to help lift you up.

C. Bring to mind people you love and absorb the feeling.

(Answer is A, B, and C.)

10. Tapping into your intuition in dating matters is . . .

A. Not overly vanilla.

B. Like budging in line, it's just out of line.

C. Fabulous, fun, and very useful. Hopefully your date is doing the same and you can connect on a new level!

(Answer is C.)

11. "Reaching through the veil" pertains to . . .

A. Making sure you are marrying the right person before the ceremony.

B. Karma. You stole mine, now I steal yours.

C. Connecting with those in spirit.

(Answer is C.)

12. Chakras are . . .

A. Swirling circles of energy throughout the body.

B. The new neighbors last name. They are from Woo-Woo Land.

C. Past-life regression pills.

(Answer is A.)

13. Seeing numbers in double, triple, or quadruple form . . .

A. Is a sign that there's a winter solstice event at the local Chakra station so it's a double-coupon day.

B. Intensifies their qualities.

C. You must have taken the "Getting Stones" chapter title a little wrong.

(Answer is B.)

14. Signs of your intuition in action are . . .

A. Everything seems to be moving in slow motion (and you are not on recreational drugs).

B. You've noticed dust bunnies under your bed and they move seemingly on their own.

C. You feel directed—as if by a tide in the ocean—to follow a certain path.

(Answer is A and C.)

15. Like a homing device, the soul *can* find its way to the One Universal Light. We just have to let our soul do its thing. Which is . . .

A. Drink lots of soul-juice every day (freshly squeezed and organic, please).

B. Act spirited and throw our hands in the air like we don't care.

C. Jump on our high-flying vibe.

(Answer is C.)

16. Reading a book like *The Happy Medium: Speaking the Language of Intuition* is good for the soul because . . .

A. Learning to understand the language of intuition gives voice to your soul.

B. When intuition is on your side, it helps you graciously and confidently stand up for what you want.

C. When we are comfortable with the language of our intuition we can just breathe and believe.

(Answer is A, B, and C.)

It's been a pleasure to write *The Happy Medium: Speaking the Language of Intuition*! Thank you for reading. If you haven't already read it, pick up your copy of *The Happy Medium: Awakening to Your Natural Intuition* and keep an eye out for the next book in The Happy Medium series.

Be yourself. Fill yourself up with light and fly!

Acknowledgments

My profound and unending love and appreciation goes out to my amazing and beautiful family, Jason, Cole, Aaron, and Sophia Rein. Thank you for believing in me and for the absolute magnificence of your love.

There are so many exceptional people I wish to thank who have stood by me in the past years as I moved, once again, through the wonders of the writing process. From longtime friends and families in the community to those I've met through my work, I am so grateful. Though the complete list is unending, I do want to say a special thank you to Michelle Bloom, Annie Wilder, Amanda Tadych, Jacque Rosenau, Debbie Orenstein, and Gary Mantz.

Much gratitude is extended to everyone at KSTP TV's *Twin Cities Live* and also to the entire staff at Beaver's Pond Press, including Hanna Kjeldbjerg, Athena Currier, and Lily Coyle.

Lastly, my heartfelt gratitude goes out to every kind and curious soul who is willing to delight in their own sparkle and thus ignite the light everywhere!

About the Author

Jodi Livon, The Happy Medium, is an accomplished medium with over thirty years of experience. The founder of The Intuitive Coach LLC, she is an intuitive coach for the business sector and offers corporate coaching, private readings, and inspirational presentations on a national level. Livon is a prominent local and national radio personality and is the resident psychic on a successful television show in the Midwest, *Twin Cities Live*.

Her first book, *The Happy Medium: Awakening to Your Natural Intuition* (Llewellyn, 2009), received a number of accolades and was described by *Publishers Weekly* as " . . . a solid and measured discussion that may give skeptics a reason to reconsider." Amanda Nieves of Edgar Cayce's A.R.E said, "This book serves to fulfill Edgar Cayce's belief that everyone can be psychic as psychic is 'of the soul . . .' If you think you may have a gift for intuition, divination, or after-death communication, then *The Happy Medium* was written for you."

Livon resides in Minneapolis, Minnesota, with her husband and their three children, a dog, a turtle, and a fish. To contact Livon for speaking engagements, online classes, private readings, or corporate coaching, visit her online at www.theintuitivecoach.com.